ISBN 1 874538 27 1

Published in the U.K. by
Old Bakehouse Publications
Church Street,
Abertillery, Gwent NP3 lEA
Telephone: 01495 212600 Fax: 01495 216222

Made and printed in the UK
by J.R. Davies (Printers) Ltd.

Contents

Foreword   v

Colour Plates   viii

Chapter I   Early Days   1

Chapter II   Towards the Limelight   11

Chapter III   From Strength to Strength ...to Disaster   28

Chapter IV   The Horn Wars   47

Chapter V   Precarious Finances   52

Chapter VI   A Question of Policy   62

Chapter VII   Up to the War   73

Chapter VIII   The War Years   82

Chapter IX   Expert - The Post War Years   87

Chapter X   E.M.G. - The Post War Years   93

Appendix I   Soundboxes   107

Appendix II   Horns   109

Appendix III   Acoustic Machines   109

Appendix IV   Cascade Machines   114

Appendix V   Select List of Patents   124

Acknowledgements   125

Index   127

List of Illustrations   129

Foreword

This story comes to be written only because a strange set of coincidences seemed to fall into place, one after the other, like levers in a high security lock, opening a door on a subject that for far too long has remained closed.

I came across my first E.M.G. nearly 25 years ago, where all treasures should be found, in the attic of a friend's house. It had belonged to his father. I fell in love with it at first sight, developing a fierce passion for it. However, it was not for sale, and not likely to be as it was a family heirloom. My disappointment knew no limits. For several years, every time I drove past that house, feelings of deep longing persisted. The image I cherished of it in my mind, seemed to improve with keeping, and over time, this amazing machine assumed a sort of mystical beauty. I could only speculate about what sounds of ineffable purity might issue from its mighty horn, if I could only get hold of it, and put it to work. One thing was certain, it was not doing anyone any good dumped in that dusty attic.

Some years passed, and circumstances so conspired that when my friend was looking for a studio to buy, I had one for sale, and he bought it. Repairing this studio ate up large quantities of old oak, for it was timber framed. When he ran out of supplies of oak, by another twist of fate I happened to have some. None of us had any money in those days, and it did not worry me at all that months went by after all the oak had been built into his building. Then, on one blissful day, he appeared on my doorstep, and asked if I would like to have the old E.M.G. in lieu of payment? It was one of the best things that had ever happened to me. At last I was to be united with the object of my desires. I knew nothing about the firm of E.M.G., and had very few records, but when, for the very first time it played for me, I heard music as I had never heard it before, and I knew, with absolute certainty, that this was a love affair that would last a lifetime.

Some weeks later, by another extraordinary coincidence, I completed the purchase of an eighteenth century warehouse in Marlborough, which had been the town's morgue. I was to convert it to a baronial residence for a customer. I had noticed that there were various piles of dusty clutter lying about there, but I had not paid much attention to them. When I had taken possession, I took the opportunity to inspect the perks that had come with the building. There was a large arched brick vault under the building, and peering into this with a strong flashlight, I saw an old hand drawn coffin bier, completely covered with white cellar fungus. It was as dramatic a picture, as any creation of Hammer Films. Otherwise, in this vault, there was nothing that rot had not consumed. However, the next floor looked more promising. Removing piles of sacks from one of the heaps, I could not believe my eyes. There in perfect condition was another Xb E.M.G. Enquiries revealed that this had been used for playing records at village dances throughout the war years, until its ancient Garrard induction motor had given up, and it had been abandoned some thirty years before. Because I was so very busy then, I was a bit slow in trying to find out if E.M.G. still existed. This was in 1980. By the time I did get round to asking Directory Enquiries, I was told that though a number was listed, the firm had gone out of business some weeks earlier. I was too late.

Marlborough was well known for its antique shops in those days, and we had a lot of dealers amongst our friends. This too was to have an unforeseen significance.

In due course we moved to Herefordshire. One Sunday afternoon the telephone rang. It was a dealer friend from whom we had not heard for some years. He was in difficulties. He was just about to go in front of the cameras on a televised antique show in London, and he was going to have to value an E.M.G., and had to have a potted history of the firm. Could I help? I told the pathetically small amount I knew, but as to value I could not help, of the two I had, one had cost a pile of oak, and the other came for nothing. I did remember just in time that I had heard of one for sale in a local auction room for £390. This seemed to satisfy him. More than a year later, he rang again. He had come across another E.M.G. in the course of business, and thought I might like to buy it. Was I interested? I asked for a description, and then, much to his amazement, asked him to play it down the telephone. He wanted to repay the favour of getting him out of his hole a year before. As the price was very reasonable, and it sounded, even down the telephone bright and clear, I bought it unseen.

When finally it arrived it was not at all what I expected. Though clearly it was closely related to my E.M.G.s, everything about it was different. The case, the tonearm, the soundbox, the horn - all were slightly different. Even more interesting, the case bore a small enamel label with the legend, 'E.M. Ginn, 55 Rathbone Place, London.'

Realising just how little I knew about these machines, I then started to search for published information. This is quite an undertaking for a farmer living remote from civilisation. Outside the small and intimate world of the gramophile, there was then little published that was easily available. I did manage to find out that there was no published history of the firm. This seemed very odd, bearing in mind the extraordinary quality that these machines clearly represented. Odder and odder!

In the course of my desultory and intermittent search, I did manage to gather some small snippets of information about E.M.G., although much of this was contradictory. I found out that these were the finest acoustic machines ever made, which came as no surprise. I discovered that the letters E.M.G. stood for E.M. Ginn, who founded the firm, but then left it in mysterious circumstances, only to start up a similar firm a little later. I was told by people who knew much more than I did, that the circumstances of Ginn's departure were still a complete mystery, and were now likely to remain so for ever.

I cannot resist a good mystery, and this suddenly seemed to be one worth unravelling, if I could. From discussions with others, I realised that I was not the only person who was interested in this puzzle. With my curiosity raised to fever pitch, with my resolve hardened, I now set out to find out everything I could about E.M.G., and E.M. Ginn. I could hardly wait to see where it would all lead.

I decided to start by contacting *The Gramophone* in Harrow. Once again, such unbelievable good fortune attended me that I began to feel as though I was being nudged forward by unseen powers. I had set out to make no more than a high speed search of the old file copies of *The Gramophone* from its beginnings in 1923, but when I got there, I was told that A.C. Pollard, the publishing consultant wished to see me. With great kindness he told me all he could immediately recall of the firm of E.M.G., and he could remember Michael Ginn very clearly. The early days of the firm though, were as much a mystery to him, as they were to me. When he had told me all he knew, as I was putting my notes away, he suddenly asked if there were any questions that I would like to ask. I only had one: did he know whether there were any of the Ginns still living, and if so where were they? For a moment there was complete silence, and a look passed across his face that I could not fathom. Then, very slowly, he reached into one of his desk drawers, and drew out a piece of paper. After a moment's hesitation he passed it to me saying; 'Perhaps you would like to deal with this then.' It was a letter from Joe Ginn to Mr. Pollard, saying that he wished to set down his memories of his father and his gramophone businesses before they were lost in the mists of time. The letter was dated only a short time previously. The coincidence, if such it was, was simply unbelievable.

I made contact with Joe Ginn without delay. From our very first meeting, at which we both got very over-excited, we got on well, and the process of unravelling the mystery began. As he was only a boy of eleven when the crucial events took place in which I was interested, it was not surprising to find that he had no very clear recollections. What he did have, which turned out to be of great importance, was the family tradition relating to these dire events. This sounded, even then, like only one side of the story, but it was a start. Now I had the names of the chief players in the drama, I set out to discover, if I could, the other side of that story. It took a long and disheartening search to locate the only survivor of the Daveys. He too was delighted to help, but now came a serious snag. He told me that the parties to the original dispute in 1929/30 had agreed at the time, that the true reasons for the split of E.M. Ginn from E.M.G. should never be revealed. True to their word, they took the secret to their graves. Had I now discovered why no one had been able to tell the E.M.G. story?

I tried every avenue I could think of to crack this intractable problem, but I got nowhere. Even now I cannot say with any certainty what gave me the idea to try Companies House in Cardiff to see if by any miracle they still had a file on E.M.G. To my amazement they had. Though it contained mostly details of the company's accounts and winding up, the file also contained treasure beyond price. There at the back of the file were a number of very faint typed sheets giving details of the company's formation in 1929, and including some details of Ginn's departure. If I had waited until the year 2000, the file would have been destroyed, and the secret would have remained in the grave. The information that the file yielded was still insufficient, but it was a good start. This prompted me to undertake the morbid task of searching at Somerset House for the wills of various people connected with E.M.G., particularly the Wests. I found one for Herbert West, but could not find one for his son Horace. This led me to search for him in this world, and shortly afterwards, I found him. He was the missing link, and his memories enabled me to make what amounts to a forensic reconstruction of the events of 1930. At last, the secret had been unearthed from the grave.

The story that follows is not strictly speaking a history. Because the bones of the skeleton have been put together from the pages of *The Gramophone*, I have not footnoted it. Anyone who has access to this source can readily discover by inference where to look up any references. Anyone who has not got such access would not need a footnote anyway. The flesh on the bones has been gathered from conversations with living sources and a tape of reminiscences of David Phillips of the early days of the firm. I have tried to tell it as a chronicle in narrative form. It is no more and no less than what I wanted to know about E.M.G. and E.M. Ginn. It is only offered as a book because I have been persuaded that there are others who would like to know. If they get half as much pleasure in reading this as I have had in collecting the information, I shall be quite content.

The earliest known E.M.G. March 1924 Magnaphone in Blackground Chinoiserie.

A selection of E.M.G. accessories developed between 1930 and 1950.

Chapter One

Early Days

The letters E.M.G. stand for Ellis Michael Ginn, but the E.M.G. story is not exclusively about Michael Ginn. E.M.G. were letters that came to be known and revered throughout the English speaking world because they were an abbreviation of the name of the firm that bore them - E.M.G. Handmade Gramophones. Michael Ginn founded that firm, but later left it to form another firm, E.M.G. continuing without him for the next fifty years. After the Great Schism, when Ginn left E.M.G. he continued in the gramophone business, so the E.M.G. story has a threefold theme: It is the story of E.M. Ginn, it is the story of E.M.G. Handmade Gramophones, and it is the story of Expert Handmade Gramophones, the firm that Ginn founded after E.M.G.

If this seems complicated, things will get worse before they get better! Arriving at the exact date when the E.M.G. story begins has in the past always been a matter of no little confusion. Obviously in one sense it must begin with Michael Ginn's birth, which was in Leather Lane, E.C.I sometime in 1899, but that is not where we wish to start. It is when he first became interested in gramophones that concerns us. Even this important date has been hard to establish. Michael Ginn, writing at various times in his life claimed that it was 1910, 1918, 1920 or 1922, but he was writing when the iron had entered his soul. As he would have been only eleven in 1910, was in the army from 1917-1919, and farming full-time from 1920-1922, none of those dates seems likely. With Ginn, it always has to be remembered that he was first and last a salesman, and a brilliant one at that. He used information to sell his arguments. If he had been an historian, he would have been a revisionist, altering the factual evidence to strengthen his chosen position. It was not that he definitely intended to lie, but he was not averse to being both miserly with the truth and generous with misinformation if that suited him. His brother-in-law, David Phillips, put the date, with equal conviction at 1922, but the events he gives to corroborate this, upon investigation, fall into 1924. The evidence, untainted by either of the chief witnesses, puts the date at 1923, and that is where we will start.

At this date, Michael Ginn was at a cross-roads in his life. Had it not been for the intervention of the Great War, he would probably have remained an assistant fish and poultry salesman, at his father's shop in Lambeth Walk, S.E.11. As it was, as soon as he was allowed, he left the private school he attended in Westminster in 1917 and joined the army. He was drafted into the Royal Army Service Corps. For a time he was blissfully happy. He loved service life, and rose swiftly to the rank of corporal. He became a dispatch rider literally a dashing occupation and one which indulged his passion for motor-cycles. It was inevitable that someone with his education and confidence should be chosen for officer training. This saved him from seeing action at the front. It was not until late in 1919 that he completed his training and was gazetted second lieutenant. By then hostilities had ended, so he got his commission and his demob' suit more or less at the same time. He came home to Lansdowne Crescent, Hove, to his wife of 1918, Esther, and their first child Joe.

This brief taste of life as an army officer had given him an appetite for command, which had translated itself into a desire to run his own business. The question was - what business? After the war, the government was offering training courses for many occupations, and Ginn signed up for a two year course in farming. He was joined by his wife's younger brother David Phillips, who wanted more than anything else to work with Michael Ginn, even if it meant he had to go farming. This was a very odd choice of occupation for either of them to have made. Neither liked getting their hands dirty, and they were not very good at farming either. Their farmer tutor, at the end of their first year told them, 'The only farm you will ever own will be a flower pot, and that will be full of weeds.' They completed the course in 1922, on different farms. The only reason anyone has ever been able to think of as to why they should have chosen farming at all, was that Michael Ginn was addicted to shooting, and David Phillips to fishing, and that they must have thought farming would somehow supply these pastimes in good measure.

The pull of the family business was now stronger than ever, for when Ginn had married Esther Phillips in 1918, he had married into another fish business. His father-in-law, Joe Phillips, owned no less than five wet fish shops around South London which made young Ginn a prince in a wet fish dynasty. Even so he resisted the siren voices of the safe and comfortable life and still looked for something exciting.

So, what turned his mind towards the gramophone? It had nothing to do with anything he had previously done, and to cap it all, he was almost totally unmusical. There were subtle threads that drew him towards it though.

For a start he now lived at 1, Vernon Gardens, Montpelier Road, Brighton, with his in-laws, and got on very well with all of them, specially his wife's brothers. The family was a fairly typical Jewish family, matriarchal in structure, and talented by inheritance. Mrs Phillips' word was the law, and the prophets too, for that matter. Music ran in their blood. Esther Ginn could have been a professional pianist, while her brother David was a gifted amateur violinist, playing the 'cello as his second instrument. Ben and Lew Phillips played the banjo and saxophone respectively. Their mother was an enthusiastic hostess, often giving parties for upwards of forty guests. These were entertained by the Phillips family band which would form at the drop of a hat, and if no-one wanted to dance, they would hold a sing-song round the piano.

The cheerful tunes that spilled out of Vernon Gardens were an echo of the waves of popular music which were then sweeping the country. Because they could read it, the Phillips's bought the sheet music, but most other people took their dose of the new music on gramophone records. The BBC also broadcast the new music, giving rise to an explosion of demand for records, which in its turn led to an unprecedented demand for gramophones. Because making gramophones was a boom industry just then, nobody should be surprised that enterprising young men should consider joining the boom. So why Ginn, the unmusical, impractical Ginn? The answer is that it was David Phillips who was interested in the gramophone, and had been for years. At the age of ten he had made his first attempt at building his own soundbox. He took an old cigar box and hammered a needle through the base. He taped the lid down, fixed his contraption to a crude wooden arm, and lowered it onto a spinning record. 'It worked' he recalled many years later, 'but it was ruinous to records of course.' Because serious music had become his principal interest in life, he had bought a great number of records to help him in his studies, and he had become increasingly disappointed by the standard of reproduction his gramophone gave him. The reproduction was never in any sense really musical, so it was natural for him to yearn for something better.

If it had not been for his friendship with Michael Ginn, any aspirations he might have had to try to improve the state of the gramophone would have died there and then, but these two young men together formed one of those most unlikely combinations that events often prove to be effective. Rolls and Royce spring obviously to mind. David Phillips had no more ability to form or run a business than Michael Ginn had to play the violin. He was naturally awkward with strangers, shy and diffident. He had been spoilt by his mother to the extent that he was unwilling to submit to the discipline of doing the mundane things in life. They were too tedious. He refused to accept, and therefore was adroit at avoiding, all responsibility. If it had not been for his musical abilities, he would have been a partner that few would want whilst being ill equipped to stand on his own feet.

Ginn on the other hand was first and foremost a salesman. He was ridiculously confident. When his dormitory at prep school had been haunted by a ghost uttering horripilating moans, it was Ginn who leapt from his bed and assaulted it with a cricket bat, while his contemporaries cowered under the bedclothes. He was a thoroughgoing extrovert, with absolutely no self doubts at all. He was a good organiser, quite happy to accept the ordinary tasks as the price of leadership. If he had any particular weaknesses at this time, they were his clumsy impractical nature and his ignorance of business and finance. The latter was hardly a matter of surprise, as he had never in his life had any money to manage. His finest asset was his ability to think on his feet with mercurial speed, as only the very best salesmen can, and he came to rely on this to get him out of any difficulties his inexperience might land him in.

So, David Phillips had the musical ability and the interest in making a better gramophone, and he wanted to work for Michael Ginn. Ginn had the confidence and ability to turn his brother-in-law's aspirations into a business. What he lacked in business and financial matters, his other brother-in-law Ben Phillips had, and he too wished to work for Ginn. Ben Phillips had been unlucky in the war. He had been to the front in the Machine Gun Corps but had been gassed, which left him depressed and enfeebled. Mrs Phillips gave her blessing to the idea of a family business, for she felt her sons were in good hands. The idea of building a better gramophone now fell on fertile soil.

Though building a better gramophone may have originated from David Phillips, the idea of trying to build the best gramophone of all came entirely from Ginn. All his life he had only ever wanted the best for himself - at school it was the best cricket bat. Later it was a camera. He did not want any old camera, but a Leica and only a Leica, and he got it. Later still, he wanted a bicycle. Not any proprietary brand either. He ordered one to be made by hand, with every possible gear and every accessory. It was a 'super-bike.' (When he found it was still hard work to get up hills, despite all the advantages, he gave the bicycle away in disgust..) It was this appetite for the best things in life that impelled him to try to build the best gramophone that money could buy. It was this same appetite that was later to drive him over the edge of disaster.

The world of gramophone design which they aspired to enter was in a parlous state. The gramophone had become a victim of its own success. It sold in ever larger numbers, so there had been no commercial necessity to improve it. Wilson and Webb in the introduction to their book *'Modern Gramophones and Electrical reproducers'* (1929) drew attention to the stagnation that had settled on the industry: "During the concluding years of the last century, the work of Edison, Bell and Tainter, Eldridge R. Johnson, H. Jones, Henry Seymour and other pioneers, established a technique of sound recording reproduction which has led to the broad and navigable highway of today. The next twenty five years saw but little advance; the initial impetus seems to have exhausted itself. Minor improvements there were of course, but they were mostly in the commercial application of accepted ideas."

Perhaps the best observation on the state of the gramophone in 1923 was offered by C.L. Balmain writing in *The Gramophone* in December 1923:

"The present form of the gramophone is a monstrosity forced upon the

---

An Unique Duplex Gramophone

This instrument is novel by reason that it can instantly be transformed from a horn machine to a hornless, or vice versa, by means of two part sections of tone-arm. Either of these sections fits, telescopically, into the hollow metal bracket at the back of the cabinet, and the two illustrations show the arrangement.

In either form, the machine has an elegant appearance, being made in mahogany, with piano-polish finish. The tonal effects, in either form, are of the highest class. The "Collier" latext vulcanite horn is supplied with the accessories. An ideal instrument for reproducing Edison discs, being constructed particularly to do so. Fitted with the latest Swiss and most approved double-spring silent motor, playing 4 records per wind.

Any Type of Gramophone made to order at Popular Prices.

---

manufacturers - so they say - by the twin devil 'Foolproof cheapness.' Those who have studied acoustics will have noted that the collection of glorified gas pipes which go to make up the gramophone of the present day, result in sounds which are third or fourth time echoes of the sound as produced by the diaphragm of the soundbox. That there are 'experts' (in the trade be it noted) who contend that 'reflecting angles' greatly improve the tone of the reproduction may be learned by consulting the May 1922 number of the *Soundwave*... Not being in the trade, I made numerous experiments along lines dictated by acoustics and common sense. I observed that one does not call upon a Chaliapine or Galli-Curci to improve their tones by singing through a French Horn - the folly of such a proceeding would be apparent to the meanest intelligence, yet that is what these artists are made to do by the gramophone makers.."

The commercial gramophone of 1923 then, was little better technically than that of 1900. The techniques of recording had improved vastly in those years, but their reproduction had failed to keep pace. The sad result of this imbalance was that the gramophone had acquired an unfortunate reputation amongst the musical cognoscenti. They saw it as a prostitutor of the musical arts - a sort of musical harlot. The well known novelist Frank Swinnerton, writing in a new publication called *The Gramophone*, called the readers' attention to the vast potential audience that awaited the gramophone, were it only to be better designed:

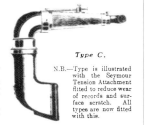

"To them, it is an infernal machine which makes all music sound as if it were played by nursery soldiers. They decry it... It cannot yet satisfactorily render the full volume of the orchestra, or the pure tone of the pianoforte. Always, the orchestra has a 'tinny' vibration, a dwarfing of the original; nearly always the piano has many notes, particularly the loud notes resembling the banjo. These defects will almost certainly be diminished in the near future. They are already less than they were a few years ago. The comparative noiselessness of the needle on the records, the reduction of crackle and hiss, the elimination of blare and bray... all are signs of the incessant search for improvement."

Amongst those who dreamed that one day the gramophone might be able to give a perfect rendering of recorded music, there would have been no dispute that the gramophone needed much improvement. To Michael Ginn and his brothers-in-law who shared this dream, the way forward along the road to perfection was by no means easily discernible. Early in 1923, they had made their first machine. This was cobbled together from reclaimed mahogany. The internal horn had been made of plywood to a design of pure guesswork, and the whole thing was made using the only tools they had, a couple of penknives, and a screwdriver. Even so, when the crude contraption first played, they were overjoyed with it, for not only did it sound much better than they had expected, but they had proved that they could in fact, assemble a whole machine themselves. As yet little information had been published that would guide them, for theoretical science had not yet been intensively focused on sound reproduction. The only handbook that was available was *The Reproduction of Sound* by Henry Seymour, and that had been published 4 years earlier.

Ginn, with unerring accuracy, decided to bypass the whole process of learning by experiment, and make a direct approach to Henry Seymour. Seymour was the one man in England who had the empirical knowledge.

The New "Collier" Patent Ebonite Horns.

Ebonite is superior to any other material for reproducing sound in connection with Gramophones or "Wireless" sets.

The exterior horn is highly finished and has an elegant appearance. The hornless type is finished dull. The latter is secured to the under side of the motor-board by screws through holes furnished in the rear end, enabling it to be suspended.

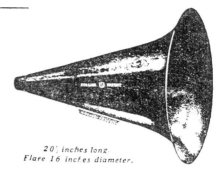

20½ inches long.
Flare 16 inches diameter.

A metal end-piece at the small end of the exterior horn makes it adaptable to most horn elbows on the market.

16 inches long.
Flare 6 × 12½ inches,

OTHER SHAPES AND SIZES IN PREPARATION.

Seymour had, by the beginning of the Great War completed the most important period of experiment and discovery. David Phillips described him as 'one of the great pioneers, following on after Edison.' He was from the same mould as many of the greatest of the nineteenth century pioneers like Davy, Faraday and Thomas Hancock. These men made many of their most important discoveries in small workshops, and on the kitchen range, but the discoveries they made in these humble surroundings were to change the world.

Seymour had been attracted to experiment in this field by his disgust at the poor quality reproduction of the machines on the market at that time. He said himself that he was literally sickened by the nasal, metallic and thin reproduction available. From the outset of his career, he had made perfection of reproduction his lode star, and he had followed this faithfully through thick and thin. His experiments had led him to make improvements in the phonograph, wax cylinders, reproducers, recording apparatus, gramophones, and disc records, matrices and master blanks. It was this broad experience of all aspects of the business of sound recording and reproduction that made him the best man to help Ginn.

By 1923, Seymour, though he still sold gramophone components of his own advanced design by catalogue, and from his shop in Caledonian Road, N7, had moved on into experiments in more recondite fields. David Phillips could recall on one of their visits to Caledonian Road, being shown the meticulously drawn designs of the Seymour Death Ray machine, which presumably derived its powers from ultra low frequency sound. This was not

Seymour Superphone 1916

what Ginn had really come to see. What was of far more interest was the machine which represented the highest peak of Seymour's achievements - the Superphone. This was recognised in the intimate world of the gramophile as the very best machine that money could buy. Seymour had once said 'You can easily magnify noise, but not quality. That's the whole thing in a nutshell.' This simple statement contains a whole world of truth, and accounted for the difference between the Superphone and the rest. It reeked of quality, and it was the search for quality that brought Ginn and David Phillips to Caledonian Road.

The Seymour household was almost a gramophone factory itself. Apart from Henry, there was Reginald Seymour, a scientific instrument maker, who was capable of making any part Henry might require, and there was Edward Vincent Seymour, who was a carpenter and joiner, should any cabinet work be required. Anyone ordering parts from the catalogue could also have a design of their own made, should they so wish. There were dozens of gramophone parts wholesalers and retailers, but the parts that Seymour supplied were recognised as the most scientific on the market. Gentlemen amateur pioneers bought them, as well as firms like the Standard Manufacturing Company (Acton) Limited who built the Vesper gramophone.

It may seem curious that a man who had devoted himself to the development of the means of improving musical reproduction should have abandoned the quest for perfection, and still be willing to help a raw beginner in the trade. David Phillips suggests one reason why this may have been so. At some stage in Seymour's career he had run into serious trouble with the two giants in the record business: "Another thing Seymour did - he used to get records recorded in those days by the Gramophone Company or Columbia. He had a very clever copying machine that he used to copy records and then market the records with different labels and with fake artists. He was doing very well until they caught up with him. He was infringing the Copyright Act, and they stopped him."

There is no doubt that Seymour had developed a copying machine, for he openly demonstrated it to members of phonograph societies who called on him in Caledonian Road before the 1914-1918 War, but until David Phillips issued this accusation in the late 1970s, no one has ever before associated record piracy with Henry Seymour. There are two things that militate against Seymour though. The first is that David Phillips was a man who was, even at the safe

The
"Superphone" Concert Sound-box
(Protected under the Patents and Designs Acts)

This superb Sound-box is a highly efficient resonating device, delivering great volume, besides giving a magnificent mellowness of tone, with perfect definition. It is fitted with a mica diaphragm.

It is generally conceded that large diaphragms have greater power and broader tone than small ones, but at the same time large diaphragms are usually deficent in "attack" by reason of their normal slow "recovery". The deficiency has now been overcome in the construction of this sound-box by the special method of clamping and highly-tensioning the stylus-bar, which has the effect of re-inforcing the diaphragm as well as promoting its more rapid "recovery".

For Concert or Entertainment work the "Superphone" Sound-box cannot be surpassed, reproducing all the vocal registers with realistic effect in a remarkable manner, whilst in the interpretation of instrumental music it is all that can be desired. It is also the Sound-box par excellence for "hornless" or cabinet machines.

This Sound-box can be supplied either with the stylus socket bored as ordinarily for steel needles, or cut with a triangular groove for use with fibre needles, at the same price. The type required should be stated when ordering, as also the type of tone-arm it is required to fit.

"I am very pleased with the "Superphone" box. I think it is worth twice as much as you charge for it. I have a collection of seven Sound-boxes, but I consider the "Superphone" the best of all. I think it is miles ahead of any other make of Sound-box " - *F.W. Smith, Esq., 4S Cavendish Road, Rotherham.*

"I have fully tested the "Superphone" box and have no hesitation in saying that this is the best I have ever heard, and I have tested all the leading makes now on the market. The results are astounding being exceptionally loud and clear in definition" - *H.C. Bannister, Esq., 42 Church Street, Barrow-in-Furness.*

"It is *the* Sound-box. especially for piano and band records, to which it imparts an absolutely natural tone. I am using it on my No. XII. H.M.V. Cabinet Grand (£46), and must say that in some cases it doubles the value of my instrument. " - *E. Chapset, L. ès L., B. ès L., Professor d'Ecole Superteure, Fourgeres, France.*

Exact Size.

distance of fifty years, terrified of lawyers, which made him weigh his words very carefully. He would not have been brave enough to make this statement unless he was sure of the safety of his ground. The second matter is the question of Seymour's obituary in *The Gramophone*. He never received one. As it is inconceivable that such a sharp-eyed publication should have merely overlooked the death of England's most important pioneer, we may reasonably conclude that this omission was deliberate, perhaps to avoid any conflict with their two largest advertising accounts, the Gramophone Company and Columbia. It is not unlikely therefore, that Seymour was deliberately keeping a lowered profile in the world of the gramophone, and Ginn's approach would have had a special attraction. By helping Ginn, he could continue to do business but under cover of Ginn's name.

Be that as it may, the Superphone was what they had called to see, and Seymour generously showed them around it, explaining the principles of acoustic reproduction, and how they were harnessed in this machine. Some insight into why the Superphone was such a superior machine may be gained from a report of another earlier demonstration Seymour gave to a reporter from the *Sound Wave* in December 1916:

"We have heard it times without number that the more we increase the volume in a reproduction, the more the true tone quality will suffer, but with the 'Superphone' this law, if it be one, has the bottom kicked out of it; and asking Mr Seymour for an explanation of this apparent paradox, he pointed out that the new Concert sound box which he had brought out for the Superphone had something to do with it, but by far the greatest factor in the case was the closing in of the soundbox and record, whilst being played. "But" we queried, "is not this a common feature of the better class of inverted horn machine?"

"Yes" replied Mr Seymour, "but the very inversion of the tonearm and horn brings about a lower ratio of volume in the reproduction per se; the ratio of surface to musical sound is approximately the same with horn and hornless machines. If the scratch is less with the hornless than with the ascending horn type of machine, it is because the volume of reproduction in the former is correspondingly smaller. In other words, the full advantage of separating record surface noises - extrinsic to those inherent in the track itself - from the general reproduction, is missed by the inverted horn principle. In the construction of the Superphone, the principle has been utilised to its fullest extent, and all the rest is deception. The Superphone has no greater volume capacity really than any horn machine would have, if operated with the same record and soundbox but it is apparently greater, for the reason that the usual surface noises are less, and the change in the relation of the one thing to the other produces this effect." We remarked that the richer tone was also probably due to the same cause, by separating so much of the mechanical vibrations from the strictly sonorous vibrations, to which Mr Seymour readily assented."

The Superphone of 1923 was to all intents and purposes the same as that of 1916, save that the horn material had been changed from Flaxite to Ebonite, and that it was now possible to have a Superphone with an internal horn if desired.

It is amusing to reflect that although Ginn and Phillips went to Seymour to further their quest for perfection of reproduction, the subsequent course they chose had more to do with the traits of Ginn's personality than with the pursuit of pure science. Ginn, because he knew so little about music and less about musical reproduction, took on the sole responsibility for the cabinet designs. His determination that his machine should have nothing but the best cabinet possible resulted in the production of cabinet models with internal horns, which flew in the face of what Seymour had taught them about the superiority of the external horn. Notwithstanding this apparent aberration, it is clear that they started more or less from the point where Seymour had stopped. Having decided on a cabinet machine, they encountered at once all the problems associated with this type of machine - resonances transmitted from the internal horn to the cabinet. Seymour had encountered these too, and had solved them by mounting the internal horn suspended from the motor board, so that, although some resonances were inevitably transmitted to the cabinet, they were not sufficient to be audible. Ginn too followed this method, and presumably with Seymour's acquiescence applied for a provisional patent for it. A number of experimental machines were built in 1923 as they gradually moved towards a design they could settle on. The machines were entirely developed from the Seymour catalogue for all their mechanical parts, they were Seymours in Ginn's cabinets. These machines were never offered to the public, but sold to the wider Phillips family. Uncles, cousins and maiden aunts, not one was allowed to refuse, and in this way like many other small family businesses, their little enterprise grew to its precocious maturity. During the tortuous process of ironing out the final faults in their designs, they were obliged to consider the important question of what they should now call their machine. It was generally agreed that Ginn was the head of the business, and that the machine should somehow carry his name.

However, Ginnophone sounded vaguely ridiculous, and did not convey the gravitas they were looking for. They had better luck when they began to play around with Ginn's initials. As a baby, he had been named Michael Ellis Ginn, though he liked to style himself Ellis Ginn, like his father. Starting with the initial of M.E.G. it is likely they moved through a predictable progression - MEGaphone (already in use) MEGnaphone - (too close to MEGaphone) - to MAGnaphone, which is what they settled on finally. David Phillips observed, many years later: 'Today it sounds a bit corny, but then it was a jolly good name.'

(The garage behind No 1 Vernon Gardens, where these machines were assembled, backed onto Windlesham Avenue. The machines made in Brighton carry an ivorine plate bearing the legend E. Ginn, Windlesham Avenue, Brighton. The machines built in that garage are by far the rarest of any built by Ginn and his brothers-in-law. If there is still more than one chinoiserie cabinet in existence, no-one has seen it since Ginn's death, by which time it had been converted to an Expert Senior. Not a single example of a Brighton built mahogany Magnaphone has been seen for many years.)

By the early weeks of 1924, they had settled the last details of their design, and were ready to offer it for sale. Now though, they ran up against a snag. It had been Joe Phillips' way to take cheap winter leases on seaside properties, so that his family could overwinter away from the smogs of London. The lease on Vernon gardens was due to expire at the end of March, just as they were ready to launch the Magnaphone. Anybody but Ginn would have put off the launch until they had re-settled in London. Not a bit of it. There were two weeks in which to test the market, and he grabbed this opportunity. Mrs Phillips lent them her drawing room, Ginn placed an advertisement in the *Brighton and Hove Herald*, and they were ready.

Advertising was an art which Ginn was to develop and refine over the coming years, but if he was in any doubt as to the effectiveness of his first attempt, he did not have long to wait. Before the paper had even gone to press, a reporter had appeared on the doorstep to investigate the 'Marvellous Magnaphone'.

IMPORTANT.

The above sketch is an impression of a wonderful new Gramophone

The Marvellous Magnaphone

Invented by a resident in Brighton and made throughout in Brighton. This machine must not be confused with the ordinary Company made Gramophones which are made by machinery and produced by mass production. The Magnaphone is a high class, hand-made machine; each one is an individual masterpiece; every point has been carefully thought out, with the result that beautiful clear music, such music, that you never thought a Gramophone was capable of producing, is now placed within the reach of all. You forget you are listening to a reproduction. the actual living artist or orchestra is brought to your own room. If you are interested in music of any kind, you must hear this wonderful machine. Being the inventor, maker and producer, I can cut out all trade profits and offer this machine at less than half the price charged by shops for a much inferior model.

The machine will be introduced by **Mr. E. M. GINN**

And demonstrated by **Mr. D. PHILLIPS**

At No.1, Vernon Gardens, Montpelier Road, Brighton
(By kind permission of Mr. J. Phillips), every day from 2.30 p.m. to 9 p.m.

The object of these demonstrations being to introduce the machine to the Brighton public prior to Showrooms being opened in London. Call any time at your own convenience. You will not be asked to purchase. I value the judgment of the Brighton Public in matters musical, and am content to leave the future of this machine in your hands.
I also have some beautiful examples of Magnaphones in Chinese lacquer at a reasonable price. Make a note of the address and call early.

Advertisement from Brighton & Hove Chronicle
March 1924.

"Those who take advantage of the demonstrations commencing today at No 1, Vernon Gardens - and advertised elsewhere in this issue - will have a satisfying taste of what a Brighton Inventor has achieved in the direction of the perfect gramophone.

The inventor is Mr E.M. Ginn and his instrument is called the Magnaphone. Mr Ginn has other successful gramophone inventions to his credit on the market but the Magnaphone which he is now demonstrating is a veritable king of gramophones, and embodies some entirely new principles.

The Magnaphone is an extremely handsome cabinet, mounted on legs, and whether in beautiful lacquer work (of any colour to suit a particular room) or in handsome mahogany, it is distinctly ornamental. Far more than that however, its reproduction seems to be as near perfection as one could conceive. It is literally a musical instrument.

A very important feature of it is the sound expansion chamber, made of special ebonite alloy, perfectly rounded and gradually tapering out from the soundbox to the large opening. It is so skilfully mounted that at no part does it touch the woodwork in any way, a feature that prevents any vibrations being heard except the pure vibrations of the music itself. The motor is silent and the table steady, and the tone arm is so delicately balanced that there is no wear of the record. Consequently the working of the instrument involves no hum or hiss.

Originality of invention and expertness of workmanship are the keynotes of the new gramophone. The cabinet is entirely handmade and is beautifully solid. The fine lines and beautiful designs of the lacquerwork are delightful, for the craftsmanship is exquisite. Every part of the machine is accessible. It may be added that the price, either in lacquer or in mahogany is very substantially less than that of many super gramophones. Those who visit the demonstrations will be able to hear - as the representative of the *Brighton and Hove Herald* has heard - how all these factors combine to produce a purity of tone that calls for unqualified admiration. A powerful Italian tenor, a deep rich English bass, a pianist of chaste delicacy, a violinist with the loveliest of sweet singing, English and American dance orchestras... found the Magnaphone a reproducer of the finest and most delicately attuned sensitivity.

The sibilants of the singer (always difficult for the gramophone) the touch of the instrumentalist and the cohesion and yet the individuality of orchestral players, all found the Magnaphone astonishingly faithful. Its remarkable clearness in the rendering of orchestral music enabled the clearest definition to be obtained of the individual contributions to the mass and colour. The peculiar quality of each instrument was beautifully heard."

As he carefully re-arranged the furniture in Mrs Phillips' drawing room, Ginn might be forgiven for being really proud of what he saw there. He had provided two demonstration models, which now faced the row of chairs. One was quite spectacular. It was a large lacquered cabinet, decorated in black ground chinoiserie, and next to it stood the standard Magnaphone model, in solid mahogany. Unfortunately, this was bright red, which was not what they intended. Thinking to save themselves money, they had ordered the cabinet from cabinet maker Mr Bradley, unpolished. After all, it was simple enough to apply French polish, wasn't it? It was not. The more coats they applied, the redder it got, until it ended up as red as a tomato. They had neither the time nor the money to replace it so it had to serve as it was. They would get over the problem somehow. It was not the impressive appearance of his machines that would have filled Michael Ginn's heart with pride. It was the sound. He had spent his money wisely, and now he knew it. Any doubts he might have harboured about the value of using the best components, had long since been dispelled. His machines sounded wonderful.

When the doorbell rang for the first time, and Ginn found the Mayor of Brighton on the doorstep, a lesser man might have been intimidated. Not so Ginn. He ushered him into a chair as though he was quite accustomed to conducting celebrities to his demonstrations. The mayor was given a personal demonstration, Ginn doing the commentary pointing out all the special features of his machine while David Phillips wound the handle, and put on the records. When it was over, the mayor approached the machines with some curiosity. Looking at the mahogany model, he congratulated Ginn on its performance, but added dubiously, "but what an extraordinary colour!" Ginn spotting the opening with the swift perception of the born salesman replied, "Ah yes. That's the modern idea. It's modern art!"

It was done so smoothly, and with such conviction that the mayor found he had bought the machine, before doubts had time to cloud his judgement. It was their first sale to a member of the public, and to an eminent person at that. It was an auspicious start.

The response to their advertisement, no doubt enhanced by the news that the mayor himself had been their first customer, was most encouraging, and far better than they had dared hope. David Phillips, typically using a fishing analogy explained: "We had shoals of people come along, and we took orders right and left."

It was during one of these demonstrations that something occurred on which they were to dine out for years to come. It was their practice to use particular records to demonstrate the amazing versatility of the Magnaphone: a piano solo to show off the reproduction of the piano, a Kreisler violin solo for the violin and so on. Then the demonstrations gradually built up from records of single instrument solos, through to vocal records, until the final climax was a full orchestra in full song. On this occasion they started as usual. Their first record was a delicate piano solo of L'alouette. Whilst the record was turning Ginn noticed a rather stout lady sitting in the front row who appeared to be either in deep concentration or asleep. She gave no sign of animation when the record finished. However, when David Phillips put on the second record, which was a violin solo, the lady suddenly sat bolt upright, cocked her head, and listened intently. The moment the record finished she implored them to repeat it at once. Rather mystified they obliged, watching her closely all the while. When the record came to an end for the second time, she fell back in her chair exclaiming "Well, just fancy that, I have just paid a fortune for a pianola, and it won't play violin at all. This machine at this price will play piano and violin!" Another sale was made.

Due to the continuing high level of interest shown by the public, the demonstrations were extended for another, positively last week. The front door had hardly closed on the last visitor, before pantechnicons arrived to move the family back to London.

The Brighton experiment had been a resounding success. The Magnaphone even though it was really a Superphone in a better quality cabinet, had proved itself able to charm the money from the public's pocket, with some help from Ginn. They had proved that they really could design and build machines to a high standard, as long as they kept Ginn out of the workshop. They could sell them direct to their public by means of direct advertising, and make a respectable profit as well. Their success had been a victory of sound science over guesswork, and hand built quality over mass production. They were now in business. The Brighton experiment had given them a good springboard from which to launch their products onto the wider market in London, where they would face a sterner and more critical test. Would the more discriminating London public give the Magnaphone such an unqualified welcome?

Chapter Two

Towards the Limelight

The Magnaphone Company, as they now grandly styled themselves took the best premises they could afford, with their very limited budget. It was not the ground floor showroom they would have wished, in the musical heart of the city. Instead, it was a large single room, above a gentleman's outfitter called Bourne and Tant, at 267, High Holborn. It was inconvenient for the gramophone makers, as everything had to be manhandled up the stairs. It was inefficient as a showroom, for it had no window onto the street, but it did have one merit - it was cheap.

When they were talking amongst themselves, they referred to their room as 'The Office,' but when in company, it was known as The Magnaphone Works, which conjured up a grander image altogether.

At this early stage of their London adventure, it was probably still a matter of debate amongst themselves whether they would sell direct to the public or through other outlets. They were still proud of their association with Henry Seymour who was specifically mentioned in their advertisements as their sponsor. They placed a Magnaphone in his showrooms in Caledonian Road, which he promised to use as a demonstrator.

They could not have chosen a more auspicious moment to open a gramophone business in London.

The Gramophone magazine, edited by Compton Mackenzie, had barely completed its first year of publication, when the Magnaphone Company opened in High Holborn. Starting tentatively as an 'organ of candid opinion,' whose critical policy would be 'personal, honest but not infallible', it soon became the focus of interest for gramophiles first in Britain, and soon afterwards, the whole of the English speaking world. In its early days, it gave opinions on the musical quality of records, the technicalities of singing, chamber music, recording techniques and reports from the gramophone societies that were springing up everywhere, but much more significantly for the Magnaphone Company, it carried advertising. Where better then to advertise? They had already decided on the *Soundwave* to which Henry Seymour was a regular contributor

267 High Holborn WC1

Even before they had had a chance to file their first advertisement in *The Gramophone*, they read that the magazine was to sponsor an open competition which all their advertisers were invited to enter. This was to take place in the Steinway Hall on June 14th, 1924 at 7.30.pm. The purpose of the competition was to test the overall versatility of the machines entered. The adjudication was to be carried out by a panel of musical experts. and also, the audience itself. Medals were to be awarded to the winners. There were to be two classes, Class I would be for machines costing up to £25, while Class 2 would be an open class.

It was typical of Michael Ginn that, even though he was not yet an advertiser, he should leap at the chance of publicity for his new creation. There were no self doubts here about what would happen to it if it was savaged and torn to bits by critics and audience alike. He believed in the Magnaphone, as every good salesman must believe in his product, and that was that. His eyes were set on the medals, and the subsequent publicity that was at stake. The proceedings were reported in *The Gramophone*.

"The informal orgy at the Steinway Hall on Saturday evening, June 14th, was, even as an entertainment a very great success, and its implications a most astonishing proof of the vitality of the gramophone movement. Every seat was bespoken many days before, and when the audience assembled at 7.15 pm. on a fine summer evening, a glance was enough to ensure the onlooker that they did not comprise the Four Hundred elite of the gramophone world, but represented a huge public which was prevented by circumstances from taking part...

The stage was hidden by a long line of screens. In the centre was a square gauze covered aperture, through which the machines played in turn. In Class 1, for gramophones under £25 retail, there were seven entries. After the test records had been played on Mr Balmain's gramophone (which he has made for the editor..) in order to establish a

Ginn's first advertisement in The Gramophone, *June 1924.*

standard for marking, the first record, the Adagio from the Spring Sonata in F major (Beethoven) was played by each machine, the order being arranged by lot; then the second record, the second part of the Aeolian Symphony Orchestra version of L'apres midi d'un faune (Debussy) which one humorist called L'Apres midi d'un gramofaune, was played by them all in a different order; the third, the Quintet from the Mastersingers. This was a test of the audience as well as of the gramophones - a test of concentration and discrimination which can hardly be exaggerated; and when it was over, the evening's work was only half done."

After the interval when a demonstration was given of the Welte-Mignon Player Piano, the judges took their places again in the centre of the hall.

"There were eight entries for Class 2, the Open Class, and wisely only two records were attempted, the first movement of the Mendelssohn Trio, played by Sammons, Warwick Evans and Mrs Hobday, and the mighty duet Brunnhilde yields to Siegfried of Austral and Tudor Davies. If there had been time, Stralia's exacting record of 'Ocean, thou mighty monster' would have been added. But there was not time; a good many of us had trains to catch, and the Mendelssohn and Wagner records were ample for judging purposes.

When that was finished the screens were removed, the judges retired, and the audience settled down... the hush-hush atmosphere of the tests had been removed, and Mr Balmain's rather uncouth gramophone was examined eagerly by the experts, while he explained the principles on which he built it.

With the return of the judges, and the announcements of their findings by Mr Kalisch, the proceedings came to an end, and it only remained for the Editor to thank everybody, judges, competitors and audience (and Messrs Steinway) for their various contributions to the success of the evening. It was very nearly Sunday morning".

The final results, which included the votes of the audience were to reveal that in Class 1 the Magnaphone had come fourth, but in the second class it had come second, and won the silver medal. Even better, Compton Mackenzie decided to aggregate the scores, and this put the Magnaphone in second place overall, for which he awarded it personally a further silver medal. The advertising value of winning the silver medal overall far exceeded anything that Michael Ginn could have dreamed of. At exactly the moment when there was a great resurgence of interest in the musical quality of reproduction, the Magnaphone found itself, through Ginn's adventurous policy, under the spotlight of public interest.

The E.M.G. Handmade Gramophone.

PERFECT IN EVERY PART.

Every Machine Handmade Throughout, no Mass Production.

Awarded the Silver Medal at the Steinway Hall Gramophone Tests.

CABINET.—Extra heavy, solid Mahogany, no ply or panels used, giving perfect rigidity.

TONE ARM.—Specially made for this machine by Mr. Henry Seymour, fitted with spring balance and special tapered base.

SOUND BOX.—Specially made by Mr. H. Seymour, both Tone Arm and Sound Box are hand-made throughout.

INTERIOR HORN.—Specially made for this machine, under the Collier patent process, the horn is a perfect round taper, made from a special *Ebonite* alloy, and opens out in front to 16 ins. in diameter.

HORN MOUNTING.—The *Ebonite* Horn is mounted in such a manner that no part of same can touch the case, therefore the sound cannot be lost or blurred by contact with the Cabinet (an exclusive E.M.G. feature.

MOTOR.—Thorens latest and best type, extra large double spring.

GUARANTEE.—Every single part of the E.M.G. is fully guaranteed.

RESULT.—The E.M.G. will play all makes of steel needles to perfection, but the results with *Fibre* Needles are really wonderful.

THE E.M.G. SHOWROOMS, 267, HIGH HOLBORN, W.C. 1.

Open from 9 a.m. to 7 p.m. • Please write for Full List.

Also at Mr. H. SEYMOUR'S, 544, Caledonian Road, N. 7.

Special Note.—The E.M.G. will play Edison Wax Discs and Pathé Records to perfection.

MODEL B.
£25 Packed free.
Height, 3 ft. 10 ins.
Width, 21 ins.
Depth, 23 ins.

Two advertisements from The Soundwave, *1924.*

Life is however, a game of snakes and ladders, and as they stepped joyfully off the top of the ladder congratulating themselves on their cleverness, they trod on a snake. They received in the post a bombshell. Lewis Young of the National Gramophone Company wrote to tell them that the name Magnaphone was, in his opinion, and that of his

ARE YOU INTERESTED?

Perfect Reproduction of a Gramophone Record either with Steel or Fibre Needles.

YOU MUST BE, or you would not be reading the "*Sound Wave*."

LOSE NO TIME IN VISITING THE

Magnaphone Showrooms,
267, High Holborn W.C.

The Perfect Gramophone at las, tat a Reasonable Price.

Demonstrations from 9 a.m. to 7 p.m.

Also Demonstrated at Mr. Henry Seymour's Showroom, 554, Caledonian Road, Holloway, N.

Apply for Illustrated Catalogue of other Models.

THE MAGNAPHONE (B)
£25 Model.

lawyers, a colourable imitation of the tradename he had already registered 'Magnophone' and that if they continued to call themselves or their machines by the name Magnaphone, he would immediately sue them. The consternation this letter caused them can easily be imagined. They stood to lose all the publicity value they had just won, and perhaps more. Like most sensible people, they had a terror of lawyers. In understandable haste, they consulted their mentor Seymour. Not for the first time, they had by instinct gone to exactly the right man. Not only did Seymour know Lewis Young very well, and was on friendly terms with him, but Seymour himself had special experience of the problem of the usurping of registered trade names. Some years earlier, in 1921 he had noticed that The Disque Cabinet Co. Ltd who had previously only made record storage units, had now designed a gramophone to fit into one of their units, and they had called it the Superphone. As Seymour had already registered the name, and paid for its registration, he immediately challenged the name, and they contested the case in the High Court. Seymour won absolutely, and so was in no doubt as to the outcome of any litigation between Ginn and Young. Young was adamant, so Seymour advised Ginn to back down, and publish a statement to the effect that he would abandon the use of the name Magnaphone. Lewis Young was satisfied and no more was heard of the matter.

This was a serious blow, but they had little option but to comply with Young's demands. It meant going back to the drawing board though, and trying to think of an equally good name. Ginn still wanted his name in it somehow, but as before the Ginnophone sounded less than dignified. In the end, he rightly reasoned, no one could object if he was to use his initials in some shape or form. Thus, he settled on the initials E.M.G., and added 'Handmade Gramophones' to give the name more weight. All this took place between the time he entered the Magnaphone for the Steinway Hall tests, and the time he won the medals, so though the Magnaphone entered, the E.M.G. Handmade Gramophone won. The loss of publicity value was not therefore as bad as it otherwise might have been.

A further misfortune befell them in August which would have done nothing to endear them to their landlord. A serious fire broke out one evening shortly after they had left the premises for the night. It took six fire engines to bring the blaze under control but by then extensive damage had been caused to their floor and the floors above.

The sudden appearance of a previously unheard of machine at the Steinway Hall tests, like an unexpected comet in the phonographic firmament attracted the attention of *The Gramophone* not unnaturally, and Christopher Stone was sent round to investigate, and possibly present the medals. In his report, one can almost hear Ginn hovering in the background pointing out those special features of the cabinet that he had designed: "It should appeal particularly to the man who likes value for money, as, being sold direct to the public by its designer, and retailer's profits are thus eliminated, any model is excellent value. The cabinet work is good, and the design not unpleasing. A minor

Advertisement from The Gramophone, *December 1924.*

feature is that when the lid is raised, the motor board is without ledges round, and can therefore be dusted in comfort. The soundbox is of normal design and is supplied with either hornite or mica diaphragms, both of which were tested with a comprehensive selection of records. (I took my own for purposes of comparison.) The machine belongs undoubtedly, but not fanatically, to the romantic school, that is to say that its tone is round and mellow rather at the expense of definition. For my part, I should have preferred more forward tone and greater crispness and differentiation. But this is delicate ground. At any rate, if the Magnaphone did not show itself a devil for detail, it obstinately refused to blast at all my 'special bits', and it lent to the jazz record with which I finished a sonorous nobility that was most impressive."

Following this meeting between Stone and Ginn, Stone was given the sobriquet 'Vo-do-de-o-Stone' which reflected his old fashioned tastes in music. This first personal contact between E.M.G. and *The Gramophone* was to have very far reaching consequences. As *The Gramophone* grew in stature and content, so E.M.G. was to grow with it, like ivy up a wall. There was mutual admiration between the two, and Compton Mackenzie, who was at least as shrewd as the next man, ventured the opinion that 'I heard quite enough of the E.M.G. at the Steinway Hall to be confident that it is an instrument with a very big future before it.'

The ripples from these tests went on and on. *The Gramophone* published what appeared to be an unsolicited testimonial for the E.M.G. from a Mr S.C. Clarke of the Goswell Road, who had had a Ginn machine for eight months:

"There is no machine on the market to compare with it. Played with a steel needle the volume of sound is most pronounced. The tone and definition are a revelation. The effectual elimination of that tinniness would convert the most biased person to a gramophone lover. Played with a fibre needle, the tone is wonderfully mellow, with not the slightest hint of that muffled or woolly effect. The cabinet being made of solid mahogany makes the machine a most desirable one."

Michael Ginn was a most creative thinker, which was what made him such a formidable salesman, and *The Gramophone* was much more naif then than it was later to become. To say that Ginn wrote this letter might be just a touch unfair, but that he had something to do with its authorship there can be little doubt. S.C. Clarke it transpires was his uncle - the proprietor of one of those magnificent barbers shops that film directors dream of. It was all mahogany and crystal mirrors, with overhead line-shafts which powered rotary hairbrushes and other gadgets. He had been one of the first members of his large family to buy (or be sold) a Magnaphone. The September advertisement for E.M.G. also carried a further testimonial, this time from S.C. Clarke Junior. The family was clearly doing everything it could to help!

Ginn's campaign of fanning the flames of publicity for the E.M.G., by any method he could devise, was to have a consequence that was to turn out to be of the greatest importance to him. His efforts attracted the attention of Percy Wilson, then a young academic mathematician, and novice gramophonist, who had not yet found an avenue into which he could channel his abilities.

Just as a magnifying glass concentrates the rays of the sun to their fiercest intensity, so Percy Wilson was to bring the science of mathematics to bear on the design of the gramophone. He had started by picking up a copy of *The Gramophone* and had read correspondence there about the problems of needle track alignment. This was a subject of great interest at this time. Records were very dear, and if the needle had a tendency to resist the walls of the record grooves, both increased noise and much worse, greatly increased wear were the result. Wilson began to examine the geometry of the gramophone, and in a short while had produced two formulae that he thought should solve this tricky problem. Calling in to *The Gramophone* office to collect some back numbers of the magazine, he mentioned this to Christopher Stone. Shrewdly Stone asked him to contribute an article on the subject for *The Gramophone*, and this he did. From this moment Percy Wilson was hooked. This first glance at the gramophone, and its deplorable state of design, like so many glances across crowded rooms, was to lead to a lifetime's love affair.

Percy Wilson was a very thorough man, so instead of blundering about on his own, he systematically visited the small group of amateur pioneers who were carrying out all sorts of experiments in different areas of gramophone technology. There was G.W. Webb who was the head of a building firm in Sutton, Surrey. His special interest was in the design of soundboxes. He had an extensive collection of phonographs and gramophones, and a vast collection of soundboxes. His workshop was well equipped with lathes and other precision tools, so he was able to make almost any component. There was H.F.V. Little, who was an industrial chemist. His special interest was in all aspects of sound reproduction techniques, and his knowledge in this field was unparalleled amongst the amateur fraternity. There was also C.L. Balmain, the Deputy Controller of the Stationery Office, who had built Compton Mackenzie one of his conical horn machines. Finally there were Lionel Gilman and W.S. Wild, whose personal obsessions were bamboo needles and soundboxes respectively.

By acquainting himself with all these gentlemen amateurs, Wilson was soon able to gain an overview of the research that was going on at that time, and by this means, he became, almost by accident, the hub of a wheel of empirical research and artistic enquiry.

Now, a further coincidence was to help E.M.G. They were at that time advertising (somewhat optimistically it has to be admitted) that they could 'improve any gramophone, sell handmade tone arms, special soundboxes, exterior and interior horns all at lowest cost.' It was a cunning way of fishing for customers, and by great good luck, they hooked Percy Wilson. They could not have caught a better fish.

Wilson's intellect was already in thrall to the charms of the gramophone, and when his eye fell on the comprehensive service apparently offered by E.M.G., it was inevitable that he should make his way there to investigate. The chemistry of this first meeting was dynamic - each party acting as a catalyst on the other. Wilson found a mutual excitement and enthusiasm for applying science to the gramophone, coupled to the apparent ability of E.M.G. to convert theory into practice. This was an ability that Michael Ginn would have laid heavy stress on, and at that stage in Wilson's career, the connection of Henry Seymour with E.M.G., in the capacity of their sponsor, would have been sufficiently impressive to convince him that this was a firm to be taken seriously. Also, he liked Ginn and the two Phillips brothers. So, while Percy Wilson was pleased and excited to have found a firm who seemed to be able to make anything for the gramophone, Ginn's shrewd mind was equally pleased to have made contact with the one man in the small world of the gramophone who encompassed all the research findings of the amateur pioneers. He was quick to see that Percy Wilson might very well become their ex-officio research and development department.

It is perhaps hard to imagine in these days, when research and development departments stand behind high wire fences, protected by every electronic device known to man, that in the 1920s the fruits of these gentlemen amateurs were freely shared, in an atmosphere of mutual curiosity. Such was the civilised world of the gramophone then, where the quest for perfect reproduction overruled any thoughts of commercial profit. That is not to say no one derived any profit from these altruistic exchanges of information, because many firms did, and none more than E.M.G.

Up to the spring of 1925 the design of the E.M.G. had not altered since the Brighton days, but now the first fruits of the new relationship with Wilson appeared, as well as the continuing influence of Henry Seymour. Seymour had come to the conclusion that the gooseneck tone arm, with a Quincke Tube, or adjustable air chamber at the dead end, was a great improvement over the tone arm used on the Superphone, so this feature was adopted by E.M.G. Wilson, whose new found ability virtually to eliminate faults in the needletrack alignment, offered his help in the design of this new tone arm, and the result was the new pivot bearing design of summer 1925. This enabled Ginn to advertise that the tone arm of every new E.M.G. machine was 'personally set for needle track alignment by Mr P. Wilson.' To some extent, the adjustable air chamber may have deflected their attention away from the vital contribution of the soundbox to the overall performance of the machines, for experience was to teach them that any adjustments in the acoustic system were better concentrated in the soundbox than in the tone arm. However, as the acoustic system had been improved by their new tone arm, the deficiencies of the Seymour soundboxes now became apparent. They had for some time been aware that the Seymour boxes lacked punch and definition. Here Wilson was able to guide them by bringing to their attention the

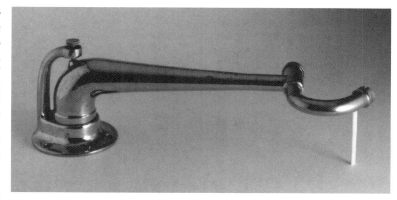

Seymour/Wilson pivot bearing tonearm, 1925.

results of the experiments of the other pioneers, and so began the long process of their own experimentation to find the ultimate soundbox. They had hoped to have produced their own design for the Gramophone Congress, scheduled to be held at the Caxton Hall in July. In this they were disappointed, and they were obliged to offer a choice of two boxes - the Luxus, and the Jewel. The Luxus soundbox was of a conventional design, with a mica diaphragm, while the Jewel was a horizontal box, designed for playing Edison records.

Adverts for Jewel & Luxus Soundboxes.

Like its predecessor, the Gramophone Congress was a competition for machines, but this time the event also comprised a large trade exhibition as well. To everyone's astonishment, over 2000 people came through the doors that day and wandered round the trade stands. "The E.M.G. stand" reported *The Gramophone*, "faced the entrance to the hall, and seemed to waylay everyone who came near it. These beautiful models had the distinction of only being sold retail, which may account for their popularity with amateurs; and the E.M.G. scored notably in the demonstrations in the hall. Mr Ginn, the only begetter of them, was much in evidence."

E.M.G. stand Gramophone Congress 1925. Left to right Joe Phillips (Junior), Harry Burden, David Phillips and Michael Ginn.

Unlike the Steinway hall tests, the audience was entrusted with the decision of which machine, in its sole opinion, was the best value for money. Competitors could choose their own records for the first demonstration, but had to play ones chosen by Compton Mackenzie, for the second. This time E.M.G. won the bronze medal, Compton Mackenzie making the shrewd observation: 'My own opinion is that both the Apollo and the E.M.G. were hampered by the soundbox they used. The Luxus is essentially a compromise...' The Orchosol won the gold medal this time, and Ginn would not have missed the fact that the Orchosol stand also sold records and accessories.

The atmosphere of sporting rivalry and general bonhomie engendered by these tests was marred by a letter which appeared in the next edition of *The Gramophone*. It came from a Mr Creese. 'The test had been a complete farce' he claimed. 'Superior cabinet work, correct needletrack alignment and fibre needles had all been completely ignored.' These particular features were of course unique to the E.M.G., and any one who might have suspected that this letter was intended for another free plug for E.M.G. would have been exactly right. Mr Creese was very closely connected with the Phillips family, and was to maintain an ever closer relationship with Michael Ginn as the years passed. His father had just sold his motor garage in Dulwich to Joe Phillips, and he was very friendly with Ben and Lew Phillips too. Once again rather unusual methods were being employed to bring E.M.G.'s name before the public. On this occasion, because Creese's voting card could be tied up to his letter, Compton Mackenzie was able to make the connection. This brought a firm but remarkably gentle rebuke, and the ploy was never used again.

Capturing only the bronze medal at Caxton Hall acted as a sharp spur to Ginn. He wanted to be responsible for producing only the very best. It was time to design a new machine.

The way their minds were working is luckily exposed in an essay which Ginn produced at this time, entitled 'Mass Production And The Gramophone.' by E.M. Ginn, 267, High Holborn.

'There is a lot to be said in favour of mass production applied to many of the necessaries of our modern existence, in fact, if it were not for Mass Production the popular cheap and reliable motor car, among many other things, would not be possible, and it is only in the production of an article which must express its own individuality that Mass production fails. We will take for example the Gramophone.

For over 25 years the Gramophone has been with us more or less in its present form, improvements have come along in the various mechanical details, but many machines of, say, 1910, can more than hold

Bronze medal won by E.M.G. at Gramophone Congress 1925.

their own in quality of reproduction - especially when carefully adjusted and slightly altered by an expert who is able to give the machine personality - with the most modern production before the public today. My readers will naturally ask why this should be so, and really, the reason is a very simple one, i.e., the so called advance is along mechanical, and not personal lines. The Gramophone is, or should be, a musical instrument, and the only way to produce such an instrument is to make every single part by hand. It is no more possible to build a real Gramophone by machinery than it is to build a Stradivarius Violin in a factory. Of course, no big maker with a modern factory can afford the time and trouble necessary to produce a Hand - Made Gramophone. It would not be a paying proposition, but a small maker can build a machine entirely by hand, test and tune the same to the requirements of each individual customer, and strange though it may seem, sell a Hand-Made Gramophone at a cost considerably less than that charged by the big Mass Production Firms. Such a firm is E.M.G. Hand-Made Gramophones of 267, High Holborn, W.C.1, who for many years have specialised in the manufacture of Hand-Made gramophones in various forms, and as the day of the individual craftsman is fast passing away, an insight into the methods of a firm entirely British, and producing an article upon the old-time methods of hand workmanship, may be of interest to our readers.

In the first place, the E.M.G. firm fully recognised the fact that many people want a gramophone that has not the stamp of Mass Production written all over it: by this I mean a gramophone that is a personal machine, tuned to the personal requirements of the actual user. There is far more in this question of personal tuning than is generally thought, for instance, a gramophone that is intended to be used for Dance music needs entirely different tuning than one which will be used by a lover of a Classic form of music, vocal, orchestral, and instrumental. The lover of Dance music requires punch, volume, and a perfect separation of all the varied instruments of a modern dance orchestra. The lover of Classical music requires all this and much more, he requires perfect purity of tone, the high strings and the low base of a full orchestra, each with its correct quality and without distortion: he requires every inflexion of the human voice, the wide range of the organ, and a real piano tone. All this can be achieved by special tuning of the sound - box, but it can only be done by a person with a very wide knowledge of this very complicated work and with an extraordinarily sensitive ear.

Again, the best records are expensive, and when used for steel needles upon the usual Mass Production Gramophone, very quickly show bad signs of wear, that is why the very great majority of gramophone experts use Fibre needles, for the simple reason that Fibre needles are harmless to the records, because owing to the fact that the material of which the Fibre needle is composed is softer than the Record material, it is the Fibre needle that wears, and not the record. A Fibre needle when used on a Mass Production Gramophone, is so soft that it can hardly be heard, but when a Fibre needle is used in a sound - box built by hand and specially tuned for this type of needle, results can be obtained that practically equal steel needles in volume of sound, and are even better than steel needles in quality of tone. E.M.G., by supplying with each pedestal machine two sound - boxes, one specially tuned for steel needles and one specially tuned for Fibre needles, give the customer a range of sound - boxes, capable of giving a perfect reproduction of the loudest Dance Orchestra or the most complicated arrangement of Classical music. Again, as regards cabinet work, nothing can equal the charm of perfectly made and finished furniture, especially when this is made by hand, as are all E.M.G. cabinets. Of course, standard designs are listed, but this design is available in every kind of wood. The standard design is not period, but is designed to tone with any period of furniture; there are no corners to act as dust traps, the whole of the cabinet is flush, so that a perfect finish to the polish can be obtained. In fact, the design relies for its appearance upon its simplicity, high-class, clean cabinet work and perfect finish. Owing to the fact that the cabinet is hand-made, it is possible to make cabinets to any correct period of furniture or antique reproduction, or to a customer's own design, in fact should a customer so desire, the maker of the E.M.G. will personally visit the customer's house and sketch a design to match the customer's own furniture. These departures from standard design can be obtained at a cost little over that of a standard model.

The various improvements which have been incorporated in the E.M.G. from time to time are the results of careful experiments, and in conducting these experiments we have received the assistance of several of the best known experts in the Gramophone World today.

It must be remembered that the E.M.G. has been awarded three medals in open competition with all the leading makers of gramophones, for purity of reproduction and quality of tone.

IN CONCLUSION. EVERY E.M.G. HAND-MADE GRAMOPHONE IS PERSONALLY GUARANTEED BY THE ACTUAL MAKER FOR TEN YEARS.'

This insight into the way they were thinking is particularly interesting as the essay itself displays some considerable confusion, and this confusion seems to have been carried over into their new models. The emphasis in the essay is on the personalising of gramophones by E.M.G., by means of soundbox tuning, and cabinet work, with very little attention being devoted to proper use of acoustic science.

By the spring of 1926 they were able to offer a wider range of machines than before, but it was a motley collection. Their flagship model was the pedestal model. As not a single one of these machines is thought to have survived, we only have a single illustration on which to make a judgement. Bearing in mind that they still believed that no part of the horn should touch the cabinet, it seems likely that they were still using the Collier flattened rectangular ebonite horn, with a plywood extension, in a cabinet of solid mahogany, but incorporating the new (Seymour/Wilson) tonearm. This represented only a minor improvement over the Magnaphone of 1924. True, there was also a new Super Table Grand model, which made use of a new 'patent alloy' horn, but, with the benefit of hindsight, this horn does not look as though it would have improved the quality of reproduction very much at all. Finally there was the Export 'portable' in teak, which was a Super Grand Table Model, with a carrying handle. This was so bulky that *The Gramophone* first wrote of it: 'The E.M.G. portable.. seemed to strain the meaning of the word though to be sure, it had a handle.' Later it was to attract a further tongue in cheek notice in *The Gramophone*: 'On a larger scale altogether is the E.M.G. portable which is only portable in virtue of having a handle; otherwise it is a table grand and a very fine handsome machine, for a fine handsome man in one of God's own countries. It was never meant for little Binks to carry from Belle Vue down to the bathing hut!'

The confusion in their minds about design criteria, is matched by the confusion in the way they were now trying to do business. Their advertisements again claimed that they would supply soundboxes, tonearms and motors, fibre needles, even a record cleaning

brush. They would undertake repairs, give expert advice, and take orders for records from all the leading makers. They would even supply equipment which would convert E.M.G. machines into loud speakers for wireless sets. They also continued to claim that they would make anything any gramophone might require. In reality, they were unable to repair anything, all repairs being subcontracted to a Mr Wenderland, a Swiss national, who had a tiny repair workshop just behind High Holborn. One is also forced to ask of what real value their expert advice would have been just now. Any technical questions would still have to be referred to either Seymour or Wilson. Their funds were now so low, that though they would have liked to carry a stock of records, they could not, so had to invite customers to place orders. The impression given by this rather unfocussed approach to business is one of a firm that had lost its way in a climate of decreasing trade. It looked as though Ginn had decided to concentrate all his efforts on getting potential customers into 'The Office.' If he could only get them in, he knew he could ensure that they did not leave before he had sold them something, however small.

The lack of direction in all their activities may be explained by the fact that early in 1926 Ben Phillips had been obliged, reluctantly, to accede to his father's request that he return to the fish business to manage one of the shops which had just lost its manager. The sudden absence of Ben Phillip's commercial wisdom was to assume an ever greater importance, as the months passed.

1926 had started full of hope and promise. Thanks to introductions from Seymour and Wilson, invitations had begun to flow in from gramophone societies in and around London for demonstrations. In February, they took a Super Table Grand to show to the East London Gramophone Society. Of this demonstration the secretary wrote:

"Of the E.M.G. much could be said, but sufficient are the plaudits thereof when it was unanimously agreed by members that, as in the case of the pedestal model, so in the case of the table grand, Mr Ginn has scored another triumph, and is undoubtedly presenting the public one of the best, if not the very best machine for tone of vocalists and instrumentalists."

This testimonial, in retrospect, turned out to be the best thing that was to happen to E.M.G. in 1926. Increasing industrial unrest throughout the country caused consternation and uncertainty, which depressed the market not just for gramophones but for everything. The new E.M.G. models had come onto the market just as the market had contracted almost to nothing. It is some indication of just how few of these models were made, that of all of them, only a single portable seems to have survived. As business activity steadily and remorselessly contracted, so E.M.G. became inward looking. More time was devoted by David Phillips to research into the soundbox question. Michael Ginn attracted some good publicity by being the first gramophone maker to adopt two new gadgets that were then being evaluated - the lifebelt, and the weight adjuster. The lifebelt was a soft rubber collar which enabled a flexible airtight joint to be made between tonearm and soundbox, and the weight adjuster was a means of reducing the weight of the needle on the record by means of a counter balance.

The year got worse as it went on. In April, they were dealt a dreadful blow. Ben Phillips had committed suicide. His worsening condition, without hope of improvement had propelled him from acute depression to this final act of despair. His loss filled them with gloom at High Holborn, but even then there was not time to grieve for long. In May came the General Strike, and Ginn who was still on the strategic reserve of officers, was called up as a special constable. At first he relished the return to some semblance of service life, but it soon paled. He was stationed in Trafalgar Square where many of the biggest demonstrations took place. The sight of women taking the hat pins out of their hats, and plunging them into the sides of the police horses filled him with disgust, and killed any passing sympathy he might have entertained for the strikers.

The summer dragged on to a rising tide of difficulties. With Ginn away, it was left to David Phillips to manage the business as best he could, and he was ill equipped to do it. Eventually the trickle of business dried up altogether. Compton Mackenzie, in his June editorial wrote:

"The gramophone industry has been severely curtailed by the strike, and the undeserved blow to prosperity coupled with uncertainty as to conditions in the immediate future, is reflected in the diminished number of advertisements in this number. We cannot complain, all must be prepared to shoulder a fair part of the burden laid on the whole community by the strike.."

E.M.G. reflected current trends. It placed no advertisements between June and November 1926, because it had no funds to pay with. When it did begin to advertise again, it was only a small notice offering deferred payments for the first time - a recognition of the desperate conditions of the market place. It was touch and go whether the firm would survive.

While Michael Ginn was helping to keep the King's peace, and David Phillips was twiddling his thumbs at High Holborn, as the commercial world was becalmed in the doldrums, events were taking place elsewhere which were soon to save the whole gramophone industry around the world from sinking into oblivion. This was the coming of electric recording.

In Britain, the first use of electric recording techniques was by Guest and Merriman who, on Armistice Day 1920, recorded parts of the service in Westminster Abbey for the burial of the Unknown Warrior. This recording, crude though it was, stimulated a series of experiments in Britain by both Columbia, and H.M.V. In the USA a parallel series of experiments was being undertaken, under the supervision of J.P. Maxfield and H.C. Harrison, by Bell Telephone laboratories. At this time, though it was possible to reproduce electric recording by electrical means, the development of the reproducing equipment was thought inadequate, and so acoustic methods had to be improved. This caused an intense study to be made of acoustic science, particularly the behaviour of sound waves. A greater understanding of how sound waves behaved led to the theoretical design of the exponential horn. The trouble then arose that to reproduce most of the ranges that the electrical process engraved into the record, a horn of no less than nine feet would be required which was an obvious non starter. Ways then had to be found, to fold this theoretical horn into a standard cabinet. All this research ultimately resulted in the appearance on the market in the USA of the Orthophonic Victrola - the first folded exponential horn model of the gramophone.

Columbia, in the USA had issued their first electric recording in June 1925, the combined voices of 15 glee clubs singing the unlikely combination of Adeste Fideles, and John Peel. The full glare of publicity into which this record was launched, almost literally electrified the market place with new interest in both the gramophone and the record. It took some time before records made by the new process arrived in Britain, and they were not received with universal acclaim. Naturally, these new recordings had to be played on outdated acoustic machines, with inappropriate soundboxes, and unscientific horns, so any criticism of them was hardly fair. This did not prevent Compton Mackenzie venting his prejudices in his November editorial:

"The exaggeration of sibilants by the new method is abominable, and there is often a harshness which recalls some of the worst excesses of the past. The recording of massed strings is atrocious from an impressionistic standpoint I do not want to hear symphonies with an American accent I don't want blue nosed violins and Yankee clarinets. I don't want the piano to sound like a free lunch counter..."

It is clear that he, like most others, had no idea of what was in store for them, when these records were enabled to release all the music that lay trapped in their grooves. H.T. Barnett, Mackenzie's friend, writing in *The Gramophone*, was not nearly so dismissive. Writing about the Columbia Adeste Fideles he wrote:

"It was given to me in great disgust by a friend on whose machine it sounded more like a complicated cat fight in a mustard mill than anything else I could imagine. I brought it home, and put it on my gramophone and the result overwhelmed me; it was just as if the doors of my machine were a window opening onto the great hall in which the concert was held. If it produces any less perfect result in your hands, blame the reproducing apparatus, and not the record."

All this frenzy of research into new recording and reproducing techniques had not escaped Percy Wilson. He too had been experimenting with horns. In Britain, the Balmain machine was considered to be state of the art, because its straight round section conical horn was thought to be the most efficient, and coupled to an Exhibition soundbox was thought to be

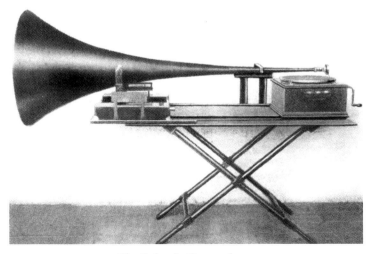

The Balmain Gramophone.

the best reproducer of all. It was also Compton Mackenzie's favourite machine. It was for this reason that Wilson wished to use it to demonstrate the possibilities of his new horn. Balmain was at that time Deputy Director of H.M. Stationery Office, and he received the suggestion that Wilson should fit his machine with the new scientific horn, with enthusiasm. Wilson supplied the former on which to build the horn, and Balmain persuaded one of the Stationery Office contractors to build the horn on it, by sticking on it layer upon layer of sticky parceltape.

As soon as the new horn had had time to dry, the entire Expert Committee of *The Gramophone* was transported to Jethou, the tiny Channel Island where Compton Mackenzie was then living, so that the members could witness the demonstration and Compton Mackenzie's reaction to it. This meeting was described many years later with understandable self satisfaction by Percy Wilson, in *The Gramophone Jubilee Book* (1973).

"We took the skeleton Balmain with us, as well as the parcel tape model of the exponential horn, and a number of soundboxes, all of which were however, designed for fibre needles. It took us an hour to set it up in Compton's library. The first record was a Sousa March. It knocked us all, including Compton, endwise. By the end of the day he was so bilious as to be positively green. He had to remain in bed for the remainder of our stay."

The sight of Compton Mackenzie having to eat his words about electric recording was payment enough for Wilson, and, as it happened, it was the only payment he was to receive, for what turned out to be one of the greatest advances ever made in acoustic reproduction. On his return to the mainland, Wilson had a cast iron elbow made so that the horn could be fitted to the HMV schools model. The former was then given to Scientific Supply Stores of Newington Causeway, who were allowed to make the horn, under the title of The Wilson Panharmonic Horn. Wilson, in his excitement, and due to his commercial naivety, failed to negotiate for any royalty, and so gained no advantage from his wonderful invention.

The decision to make this horn from layers of paper, papier appliqué, to give it its proper name, was a stroke of genius. Paper built up in this way does resonate, but at so low a pitch as to be inaudible to all but the keenest of human ears, so it was to all intents and purposes, resonance free. What turned out to be of equal importance was that this material was so cheap, making the horn available to all, at a modest price (three guineas).

The Wilson Panharmonic Horn was first placed on the market in January 1927, and Ginn, who had already heard rumours of it, hastened to buy one. Like every one else, he was astonished by its performance. Unlike every one else, he saw at once how he could use it to his advantage. Even so it took him until May 1927 before he was able to offer the first E.M.G. Wilson Horn Model, and this made him the first manufacturer to adopt it as standard. Once again, it was Ginn's unshakeable faith in his own judgement, and therefore his product that carried him forward. He was certain that the vast leap forward in quality of reproduction that this machine offered would sell it. Others were by no means as confident that anyone would readily accept a machine with a 50 inch straight horn in their houses. It was this doubt in the mind of his competitors that allowed Ginn to score an early triumph. Being the supreme self publicist that he was, Ginn not only managed to bring his wondeful new machine to the market place first, but somehow he managed to convey the impression that E.M.G. had always been in the forefront of scientific research and gramophone making, so that it was not long before the critical musical public came to believe him. Not only that, as the accolades were heaped upon them from *The Gramophone* amongst others, every one wanted to hear the new electrical recordings, and the only machine to hear them on was thought to be the E.M.G. Wilson Horn Model. Timing was almost a mystical art with Ginn. Now was the time when there was a sudden and voracious demand for a machine to play the new recordings, and here, as if by magic, was Ginn, offering the only one.

The first E.M.G. Wilson Combination.

What this machine looked like in its standard form is not exactly known, as only two examples are known to have survived, and both of them are different. Despite this difficulty we can deduce quite a lot from them. The machine basically comprised three elements; the E.M.G. gooseneck tonearm of the pivot bearing type used on the 1925 Magnaphone type E.M.G. models and subsequent ones, the Wilson horn, and the new E.M.G. soundbox. The tone arm was redesigned to match the expansion rate of the horn, and was fitted upside down, with the gooseneck reversed, so that the base of the tonearm was the socket into which the horn now fitted. This arrangement was as ingenious as it was simple, and for the very first time the whole acoustic system complied with the Wilson expansion of sound formulae. It was this balanced system which gave to the E.M.G. its great effectiveness, despite its short acoustic length.

The soundbox was a new departure. It was based on the Exhibition box, with at first, Exhibition type stylus bar mountings. The small mica diaphragm, and the almost infinite capacity for tuning gave David Phillips, really for the first time, the chance to tune a box exactly to a balanced system. It was this combination of features which made the new E.M.G. outstanding in its field. It was not at all surprising that it was greeted with unreserved delight by those who heard it play. It was simply a brilliant example of the application of pure science to the gramophone. Though the guiding hand of Percy Wilson could be clearly seen in all its main components, no one should underestimate Michael Ginn's contribution to its success... the ability to convert theory into magnificent practice, and at an attractive price too.

At 267 High Holborn, where only a short while ago, they were desperately worried about how they would find the next rent payment, and bankruptcy must have been only a whisker away, now there was frenetic activity. Orders poured in to an overflowing order book, customers jostled each other on the stairs in their haste to place orders. Those who could not quite afford the price of a new E.M.G. demanded that the firm should convert their existing machines to the new system. Here again, Ginn seemed to have the luck of the devil. Some years before there had been many people who had made the mistake of buying the ill starred HMV Lumiere machine with its curious pleated diaphragm in place of a horn. There cannot have been many people who were not subsequently disappointed with their purchase, and who were thus left with a magnificent cabinet. Now these machines, which only served as an irritant and a disappointment, could be cheaply converted to the finest reproduction system available. A great many conversions of this type were carried out, a fact which probably gave rise to the myth that E.M.G. bought Lumiere cabinets from HMV to use for their own machinery. It is true that many features of the Lumiere cabinet were later adopted by E.M.G., but that is a different story.

The sweet smell of success began to pervade their premises. David Phillips recalls that at this time they were assembling and tuning up to seventeen machines a week. So - everything in the garden was lovely - wasn't it?

Chapter Three

From Strength to Strength....to Disaster

In early 1928, the pre-eminence of E.M.G. was due principally to the performance of the Wilson Horn, but knowledge of the properties of exponential horns was not exclusive to E.M.G. In due course, as was inevitable, folded exponential horns became available in the new range of HMV cabinet models. In January 1928, *The Gramophone* published a technical report on this new range of machines, and their findings would have come as something of a shock to Michael Ginn:

"In this catalogue, the Gramophone Company lay stress on the freedom of these instruments from 'gramophone tone' and in this we think they show their usual flair, for there is no doubt that one of the characteristic features is the absence of 'nasality' with which we have been only too familiar in the past. This improvement is clearly due to the large exponential horn embodied in these new models. For the first time the acoustical system is not a compromise, but a true scientific design. Instead of the cabinet being wasted on totally inadequate record storage it is entirely given up to its proper use. The whole front represents the mouth of the horn, which, starting from this basis, is carried back by means of a most ingenious series of bends until it terminates at its small end in the tonearm. In the large (202) model, this gives in effect a horn nine feet in length, capable of producing a bass which is not merely impressive or due largely to meretricious reinforcement by horn or cabinet but is the result of a true capacity to deal with extremely low frequencies.

It will be gathered from this report that we have been greatly impressed by these instruments. In the past we have strongly advocated the open horn because it was only in this type that music and science had not been subordinated to cabinet work. Now that constructive ingenuity has been more worthily applied - it is only proper that we should be the first to applaud."

Two early E.M.G. Soundboxes

It was bad enough for E.M.G. that a mass producer of gramophones should have adopted the new science, and that the larger models had longer acoustic systems than E.M.G. What was far worse was that these new machines were cabinet models. This severely threatened the newly created fashion which decreed that only in the external horn machines could the connoisseur get the best performance.

With all the confidence that a healthy bank balance and a full order book gave him, Ginn took immediate steps to meet this challenge. He would offer a bigger and better cabinet model, incorporating the latest exponential formulae, to give an even better performance. This idea was much easier to imagine than it was to bring to reality. It would require an entirely new acoustic system for a start. Percy Wilson could be relied on to design that - or so he thought. To his horror, Wilson declined. It was a more time-consuming project than he had time to give. Had the matter rested there, Ginn would have been obliged to forget this model, and history would have turned out quite differently. Wilson though, on seeing Ginn's crestfallen face, and having some sympathy for his dilemma, took pity on him, and promised to introduce him to a friend, who might be able to help. This meeting was to have consequences that neither man could possibly have foreseen.

Horace Balfour Davey MC, or Balfour Davey as he came to be known to his friends, came over to High Holborn from Hampstead, where he had lived since coming out of the Royal Flying Corps after the war. He was so different a creature from Ginn that in the ordinary course of life they would never have expected to run across each other. It was only their shared interest in the gramophone that enabled a bridge to be built between their two different worlds. Balfour Davey was very tall, and of a slight build. He was so tall that one might be forgiven for speculating whether he had had to be folded into his cockpit like the HMV exponential horn had to be folded into its cabinet. He was so quietly spoken that the slightest noise would obliterate his voice, and his words would be lost. By nature he was retiring, and painfully shy. He was a true solitary. Most of his early youth had been spent in the company of his brothers and sister only, with little contact with the world outside the family. His father was a regular soldier who was more often away than at home - serving in India and in the South African war. He knew his grandfather almost as well as his father in the early days, the first Baron Davey, one of the law lords. He was a most cultured man, a man of the most refined musical and literary tastes, and Balfour Davey was more likely to have inherited his own musical tastes from his grandfather, than his father. His grandfather was also an influential and enthusiastic old Rugbeian, which was why Balfour Davey's father had been to Rugby, and why, in his turn Balfour was sent there too.

The only known photograph of Horace Balfour Davey.

The regimen at Rugby was famous for being hard, masculine and militaristic with sadistic undertones, and it had little appeal to this gentle musical boy. He was very unhappy there, driven in on himself by the often brutal system, but it was a testimony to his strength of character that he was not defeated by it.

On the outbreak of war, he joined the 6th battalion the North Staffordshire Regiment. He would have been twenty years old. Soon afterwards, he transferred to the Royal Flying Corps, where he was commissioned. (He always maintained that pilots were chosen for their ability to ride a horse well - balance being the chief requisite for the pilot). Once among the clouds, he found himself in an element that strangely suited him. In the solitariness, he found a peace he had never found on the ground - the vastness of the sky he found somehow comforting. Even in aerial combat, and he shot down at least one enemy plane, he was fighting on terms he understood and approved of. In the air the scale of the war was reduced to a personal duel. The dogfight though lethal in intent was gentlemanly, even chivalrous in execution. This form of warfare suited his self-reliant solitary nature.

Throughout his life, Balfour Davey was to write very little of himself, for he abhorred any form of self publicity, but we are lucky that under extreme provocation a few years later, circumstances squeezed out of him some of the reasons why he turned his attention to gramophone design:

"I designed a gramophone for the first time simply because I wished to hear my own records really well produced. I was convinced that the gramophones of that day (1926/27) were not designed and built on a serious and scientific basis. The wide disparities in constructional practice and in the performance of these made this conclusion inescapable.

The results I obtained from these small instruments which I built, surpassed my expectations, and deepened my conviction that here was something waiting for me to do. I longed to hear better reproduction than my small machine could give and to share with my fellow gramophiles the pleasure of getting really high quality reproduction at a reasonable cost. I started to design bigger machines at once, labelling my designs with Mark numbers, a survival of military ways."

Balfour Davey had been one of those amateur pioneers on whom Percy Wilson had called, when trying to amass knowledge of the gramophone himself. He must have been impressed by the machines which Davey had built and the application of good science to them, otherwise he would not have introduced him to Ginn. It had been a matter of mutual advantage for Wilson to have allowed Ginn to use his designs in the E.M.G. standard machines, for Wilson was first and foremost a theorist. He needed to see his designs made up in practice to test the practical validity of the theoretical discoveries he was making. When he could no longer provide the new designs, it would have been of real importance to him to keep E.M.G. on the narrow path of science. Davey seemed to offer this continuity. Davey was just then on a parallel path to Wilson, experimenting up to now for his own benefit, but wishing to see his designs made up. Ginn seemed to be offering him the fulfilment of his wish.

Michael Ginn, who was just beginning to realise that to be the leading scientific gramophone maker, whilst at the same time being scientifically illiterate himself made him a hostage to fortune, must have viewed the appearance of Davey as the act of a benevolent Providence. Davey with his quiet calm and unassuming presence looked to be easily manipulated. He was of independent means and Ginn almost certainly scented the possibility that he might not have to pay him. Davey was too much of a gentleman to raise the question. The arrangement they entered into, although it appeared to give both parties what they wanted, was established on a vague and undetermined basis. It was a house built, not upon a foundation, but on shifting sand. This too was to have unpredicted consequences.

The first machine to benefit from their co-operation was breathtaking, and not just because of its size. The only restriction on the design was that the cabinet must be able to pass through a standard thirty inch doorway. The acoustic system was to be the longest and largest that science would permit within this limitation. Because quality in the acoustic system took a priority over the cabinet work, Davey was able to specify ebonite for the

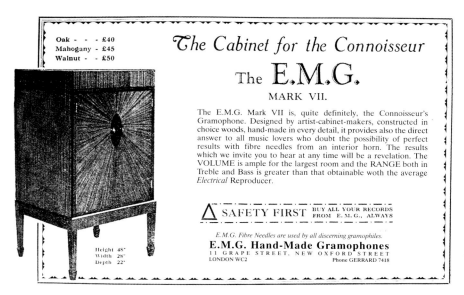

The first advertisement for the Mark VII.

horn. He invented a completely new shape of horn, suspended from the motor board by the old Magnaphone patent method, and curling round a 270 degree bend to a bell of seventeen and a half inches. To complement this he designed a new and much longer tonearm. Because the acoustic system had been so expensive, Ginn was a bit limited when he came to design the cabinet. He would have preferred to have made it from solid wood, but now cost prevented this. It would have to be plywood, with a veneer covering. Being Michael Ginn, he found the finest veneerist in London, Frank Darrieulat to do the job for him. Darrieulat modestly described himself as an 'artist in wood'. He was a superb furniture maker, and expert in the subtle blending of veneers. The resulting cabinets in walnut or mahogany were spectacular, while the oak one, the cheapest of the range was impressive but looked severe.

This machine, the first E.M.G. machine to be advertised bearing the Davey Mark number was designated the Mark VII, and was first available for sale in July 1928. The letter they received from the first purchaser must have made all their efforts seem worthwhile:

"Dear Mr Ginn. The finest gramophone in the world is owned by myself and made by you. Reams of paper and pints of ink cannot say more, as every other make is skinned alive."

Ginn claimed for this machine that it had 'a greater range from treble to bass than any other machine on the market, and this can be definitely proved.' While this was certainly what he had been aiming at, we may be permitted a small doubt as to whether this claim was strictly true, as the Mark VII had a shorter acoustic system than the HMV 202. What we can say is that the quality of reproduction achieved was simply superb, and the tone is of such a delicacy, that it is beyond the power of mere words to describe. Some people claim that this model was the finest gramophone E.M.G. ever built. Once again, E.M.G. had clawed its way back to occupy the musical high ground.

The friendly and enthusiastic reception that this cabinet model attracted, encouraged Balfour Davey to turn his attention to improving the Wilson Horn model. He would doubtless have wished to increase the length of its all too brief acoustic system, and casting his mind back to a letter in the *Talking Machine News* some years earlier he would have recalled that a correspondent had written in suggesting that this lengthening of the system might be achieved by the simple addition of a U tube under the motor board, to connect the tonearm to the horn. This is exactly the step he took, and by having the tonearm redesigned to conform to the Wilson expansion of sound formulae, so that the whole system was once again in correct balance, he managed to ratchet up the quality of reproduction dramatically. There is absolutely no question that the Mark VIII, as it came to be known, was a far superior machine to its immediate Wilson Horn predecessor. Once again demand jumped and the lights burned late at High Holborn.

The Mark VII E.M.G.

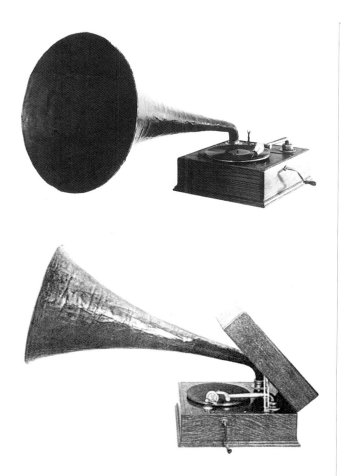

Mark VIII Standard (top) and Deluxe (below) models.

The direct consequence of E.M.G. leading the market again was that the great flywheel of commerce began to turn that much faster. The bank balance grew in proportion to the growth in orders, new customers were signing up all the time. This great efflorescence of business brought new opportunities. Broadcasting was by this time in 1928 well established, after an uncertain start. Until this time, the vast majority of wireless receivers were home built. Circuits were simple, connections were made by knurled nuts rather than solder. Valves were of the bright emitter type which shared the unfortunate twin characteristics of being both expensive and unreliable. There were no properly organised dealerships either. In the cities where signal strength was strong, it was wireless component shops which sold the means to listen in. The commercial development of the mains receiver had been severely hampered by the slow spread of the National Grid. Even seven years later in 1935, only half the country had mains electricity, and of that half 20% had only direct current.

Up to this point in 1928, Ginn's only gesture towards the wireless had been selling the gadgetry to convert Wilson horns into loud speakers, and this state of affairs might have persisted had it not been for another quirk of fate. Neither Ginn nor Phillips had at that time any real knowledge of the principles of radio, but Balfour Davey knew a man who had.

This man was Francis Granville Gordon Davey, Balfour's younger brother. He had only that summer left the army, and was in the process of setting himself up as a consultant electrical engineer, specialising in wireless installations. He just happened to be one of the leading experts in this type of technology He had arrived at this fortunate state by a

Captain Francis Granville Gordon Davey M.A.

circuitous route. Leaving Winchester College in 1916, he followed family tradition by entering the army. He first joined the Royal Engineers, graduating in 1918 from the Royal Military Academy, then at Woolwich. He was gazetted second lieutenant, and in 1921 transferred to the Royal Signals. He spent some considerable time serving with the British Army of the Black Sea, cruising up and down the Turkish coast, on a destroyer, building and testing radio communications equipment. The army sent him to Caius College Cambridge from 1923-25, where he obtained a first class honours degree in Mathematics and Physics.

In addition to establishing a consultancy, he became a partner in a company called Wireless Music Limited, with Maurice Trouton and Rupert Carpenter. This firm was to specialise in building high quality wireless and electrical installations, designed to receive and broadcast music and to reproduce that music musically. In this field, Wireless Music Limited was both a pioneer and leading exponent. Frank Davey differed from Balfour in one vital respect. He enjoyed the company of people with intellects equal to his own, and as many of these were well heeled, he tended to gravitate towards a social circle a cut above the ordinary. He was in many ways the electrical equivalent of Percy Wilson, indeed he was to give much help to Wilson over the years, including, curiously, a new formula for needle track alignment in 1929. He was by inclination a scientist, not a man of commerce, though he was no commercial innocent either. There was in 1928 no man better qualified than he to design bespoke wireless sets, capable of reproducing broadcast music well. In 1928, he shared his brother's house, and they must have discussed the possibilities. It was inevitable that E.M.G. should become wireless makers, and this they did by midsummer.

By this time, the success of Balfour Davey's horn designs, which benefited without doubt from his brother's expertise, had established for him a reputation in the small world of the connoisseur's gramophone, second only to Percy Wilson. Because of this, he was invited to join the Expert Committee of *The Gramophone*. This was a great honour, and by it he became an Olympian among gramophonists. He was now in direct contact with the other leading amateur pioneers, and party to their private research. He was also enabled to gain insights into all the technical problems that stood between current practice and perfection of reproduction, and into their possible solutions. The solutions suggested by the experts could then be taken home, and discussed with Frank Davey. This cross fertilisation between the Expert Committee and the Daveys enabled E.M.G. to straddle the gulf between acoustic and electrical reproduction, and put the firm, through the Daveys, into a position of unique advantage. The work of the Expert Committee was of course entirely confidential, until its findings were published in *The Gramophone*. but it can hardly be a coincidence that E.M.G. was to stock many of the items that the experts were later to recommend.

The firm continued to go from strength to strength. Everything at this time seemed to conspire to favour E.M.G., so perhaps Ginn may be forgiven if he took an hubristic view of his competitors. When Delius himself, then blind and paralysed, wrote to congratulate him on the Wilson Horn model, his cup must have seemed filled to overflowing.

"Dear Mr Ginn, Let me thank you again for all the pleasure I derive from listening to music through your excellent gramophone. It has a beautiful pure natural tone, and gives wonderfully clear and distinct rendering of orchestral music, as well as of the voice, so that one understands the words remarkably well. I often use it to play records of my own works to musicians who come to see me, and they all think it splendid. My wife has quite mastered your instructions, and gets on very well with fibre needles."

The seasoned observer of human affairs might have expected Nemesis not to be far away. The sky was all blue - so, where was the thunderbolt?

When Charles Kay Ogden came up the stairs at High Holborn to buy his Mark VII cabinet model he may have looked ordinary enough, but his purchase was to have consequences beyond anyone's wildest dreams, or in Ginn's case most ghastly nightmares. Perhaps if they had delivered it to his Cambridge home they might have concluded that he was in no sense ordinary, though it is doubtful if they could have prevented the disaster from overtaking them. They would have been greeted at the door by Ogden himself probably 'smoking' a cigarette which sported a glowing red electric bulb at its tip. Entering the house, they would have had to squeeze past his coffin which he kept in the hall, in case of need. Clambering over his

E.M.G. Mark VIII conversion of 1909/10 HMV Grand.

collection of eighty two family bibles, and forty two pairs of shoes, they might at last have gained access to his living room. Here, even on the hottest days of summer the windows would be tightly closed, while an ozone machine quietly puffed away in the corner giving a stream of purified air.

He was a true eccentric, an ideal frame of mind perhaps for a psychology don, and a man of extraordinary dynamism. He already enjoyed a modest fame for having invented in 1926 BASIC English (British, American Scientific, International Commercial) a language consisting of only eight hundred and fifty words. This was a successor to that invented by Ogden's hero, Jeremy Bentham. He was not so much a crazy man, as a man of crazes. When he bought his E.M.G. Mark VII, he was suddenly filled with a missionary zeal for it, and immediately set about proselytising the musical heathen in Cambridge and indeed, anywhere he had friends. His perpetual poverty, which he described as 'Hand to Mouth Disease' coupled to his new found enthusiasm for his E.M.G. caused him to appoint himself as Ginn's ex officio salesman. Ginn only sold direct to the public, but he was not averse to using one customer to introduce another. When this happened, he paid a commission, hence the attraction to Ogden. He was a first class salesman too, and Cambridge dons bought very many of these machines as a result. This was to be of inestimable value to E.M.G. in the future too, for students, seeing these wonders of science in the ownership of their dons, came to regard them as the most desirable of gramophones, and in their turn bought one for themselves.

Ogden had a wide circle of friends and acquaintances, many of them members of London clubs to which he belonged. One of those who bought an E.M.G. through Ogden was Herbert Edgar West a stockbroker. Herbert West was, in one sense at least not unlike Michael Ginn. He was a perfectionist. He enjoyed the best things in life, good food, good wine though in moderation, good pictures, good music. He set a high standard for himself in everything he did, but did not set a high store on what others might think. West living just round the corner from the Queen's Hall, was one of those people completely captivated by the new electrical recordings, who waited impatiently as the record companies slowly made the great classical works available. Ogden too shared his enthusiasm, and when a new recording came out he would hurry round to Herbert West with it so that he could enjoy it hot from the press, as it were. Ogden was a frequent visitor at Herbert West's house, and they both came to share a deep affection for their E.M.G.s.

Herbert Edgar West.

The stockbroker of 1928 was not at all the same animal he is today. A man who required capital to develop his product could not then go to his High Street bank for it. He had to find a stockbroker. This was not the straightforward matter one might think either. It was essential to find a stockbroker whose integrity was completely above suspicion. These were the days leading up to the Hatry case, which exposed a £14,000,000 fraud. To find your honest broker, you first had to find someone in the City, with an unblemished record, who would recommend to you a broker of his acquaintance. If you could persuade him of the bona fides and value of your product he would find the investors, who would put their money in on his recommendation. He would arrange the formation of the company, and matters could then proceed. Similarly the broker himself was always on the lookout for likely things to invest in. If he found a likely one, he then dared not hesitate for fear that someone else might get in first, so it was altogether an opportunist market place.

Herbert West had had his failures, as well as successes. He, along with many others had been caught by the Islas del Guadalquivir Company. He had been invited to back the Serpolet steam car company in Paris. He had gone to Paris for the demonstration. The Serpolet approached, leaking steam from every orifice. West described it later as a row of Bunsen burners on wheels. As it chugged up and down the Paris Boulevards, a crowd, doubtless hired for the occasion cheered, crying "Vive La France! Vive Serpolet!" As soon as the machine stopped, West hopped off it with alacrity, saying "Non! C'est Vive Mr West," and declined to invest.

He had been approached by C.C. Constantinescu, who had invented the Interrupter Gear, allowing a pilot to fire a machine gun through his propeller without shooting it off. West firmly believed in trying out the product himself so he insisted on being taken up in the little plane to witness the demonstration at first hand. He endured two long bursts of machine gun fire, but politely declined the offer of a third, reasoning that one can push one's luck too far, but he did arrange the finance for it. The Marles Steering gear company was another of his successes, less dramatic, but equally profitable.

Now, once again, coincidence was to play a star role in the E.M.G. story. Herbert West was at that time, a partner in the stock exchange firm Hichens Harrison. In 1925/26 a young man joined this firm who brought with him, even at his young age, a buccaneering attitude to the market. This young man was Edward Lewis. His association with Hichens Harrison was not destined to be a long one - perhaps their more cautious and conservative approach stifled him - but in this time he got to know Herbert West quite well, well enough for a frank exchange of views. It was this cross fertilisation of ideas that subsequently came to have such a great significance.

Edward Lewis left Hichens Harrison to join a new firm, which was then acting as brokers in the sale of 370,000 shares in a firm called Barnett Samuel and Sons Limited. Originally a firm of musical instrument makers and later on factors for gramophones, it had wisely diversified into making gramophones just before the Great War. By 1928 this firm was a ripe financial plum ready for picking. The sale was a thumping success and heavily oversubscribed. This firm made Decca gramophones.

Lewis reasoned that a gramophone maker which did not sell records was like a razor maker who did not sell blades. He now set out to find a record making firm which was in difficulties to complement the Decca gramophone Company. In this he was soon successful. The Duophone company which had a 75,000 square foot factory in Kingston-on-Thames was working at only half its capacity, and was struggling. When Lewis reported this to the new Decca board, he was deflated to find that it was not enthusiastic about the acquisition of this complementary business. It declined to take Lewis' advice. Within a week he had raised the necessary £145,000 and bought the Duophone Company lock stock and barrel. He renamed it the Decca Record Company.

Herbert West had watched the sale of shares in Barnett Samuel and Sons Limited with great interest, and doubtless counted it a missed opportunity. He had also watched Lewis' purchase of the Duophone Company, and understood the clear logic of Lewis' attempt to put the two firms together. Now, here was E.M.G., the most prestigious gramophone maker, with full order books, and a burgeoning reputation. West might be forgiven for thinking that he had come across a Decca situation in miniature. Here was the razor maker, perhaps the best razor maker of all but it did not sell blades. But could it, if pushed in the right direction? By increasing production of machines, and selling records, could E.M.G. not be turned into something of real commercial significance?

Like many another hard and shrewd man, sentiment lurked never far beneath the surface of his carapace. He had been known to make investments of a whimsical nature - there was the brewery in Bexley for example. He liked their beer, they needed capital, he provided it. It was as simple as that. He held his E.M.G. in the highest regard and affection so, as the idea began to shape that he might be able to turn E.M.G. into an efficient financial entity by putting money into it, there was already an element of sentiment buried in the equation.

It was C.K. Ogden dashing to and fro between Ginn and West like a bee on orchard blossom, who brought the news that West might be prepared to invest in E.M.G. This was flattering news indeed for Ginn. Things were going so well now, that it seemed only natural that others should wish to share in his success. Had Ben Phillips been still alive, a great deal more caution would have been exercised. He was not alive, so caution was not exercised.

When in due course the two men met to discuss the possibilities of the situation, it is important to remember, in view of coming events, that their competencies were worlds apart. Herbert West was both extremely shrewd, and widely experienced in matters relating to the creation of wealth, while Ginn was an innocent. This gulf was a potential hazard that Ginn did not notice. There is no doubt in my mind that West showed Ginn how E.M.G. could be re-designed as a business, so that it became much larger, more efficient and broader based. A loan of capital would enable Ginn to move to better premises in which he could combine all aspects of his business under one roof. He could open a comprehensive record business, with agencies for all the leading makes, supply books and miniature scores - in other words become a one stop shop for the serious music lover. This vision which West showed to Ginn opened his eyes to previously undreamt of possibilities. In his inexperience Ginn only saw the 'Holy City' not the rocky road through the Valley of Despair that led to it.

On November 8th, 1928 Ginn signed a loan agreement with the stock exchange company that Herbert West used for his speculative transactions, the BAW Syndicate (Brodrick and West). He agreed to borrow £5,000 repayable in ten years. The loan was made to Ginn in person, and the cost to him was 25% of the business profits computed half yearly. The purpose of the loan was to enable the firm to increase production of machines, and the scope of the business. Ginn now was able to set about re-organising his business. Unlike the penurious circumstances which faced him when he first moved to London, he was now able to seek a bigger premises in a better position, and it was not long before he found it. Grape Street, a narrow russet coloured street leading off Shaftesbury Avenue, was quiet and dignified yet ideally placed close to the musical heart of the city. Number 11, Grape Street was vacant, and Ginn took a twenty year lease on it from the Aberdare Trust.

He had several good ideas about the re-organisation. He managed to persuade Horace Hill to rent the basement as an independent engineering business. Previously Hill had worked as foreman engineer for Cinetra, who made cine cameras. Hill was a personal friend of Ginn, and he would make all the metal parts for E.M.G. on the site. The ground floor was to be given over to the new record department and audition rooms, with space for displays of machines. These would be assembled on the first floor, where the offices would also be, and Frank Darrieulat was to have the top floor for his own cabinet making business, where he would also make the gramophone cabinets.

Things began to go wrong from the start. The builders, as is the way with builders, failed to complete the alterations in time, and the opening had to be delayed by a month. Rumours then began to circulate that E.M.G. was going in for mass production. These required a public denial. These rumours

Grape Street, W.C.2

were then fuelled by the registration of another company calling itself E.M.G. Limited, which also made gramophones. Ginn was understandably touchy about names, after the Magnaphone episode, so he challenged the new company. They did agree, in the end, that they would change their name to Electrical and Mechanical Gramophones Limited, which for Ginn was an unhappy compromise, but it was the best he could get, and he was forced to accept it. All this was very unsettling and did nothing to enhance E.M.G.'s exclusive image. After only a few weeks, there was a serious fire in the cabinet making department, which nearly lost them their roof. This fire further delayed production of machines.

Eventually, the dust settled and they were able to get down to business again. To counter the false accusations that E.M.G. were going to mass produce their machines, Ginn had gone to some trouble to emphasise publicly that E.M.G. only built machines to private order. This led to strange orders, from customers who had their own ideas, and wanted to see them made up. One gentleman asked them to build his own variant of the Wilson Horn model. He required the horn to rise from the cabinet of his machine, strictly on the correct expansion formulae, travel across the ceiling of his spacious drawing room, and curve down over his favourite armchair, literally disgorging the sound over his head. The idea was sound enough, but one has to wonder if he had time to get back to his chair after putting on the record, before it was finished. Perhaps the butler put on the records. Another order was received from C.K. Ogden. Not content with a gramophone that played records conventionally, he now required a machine that would play them backwards! Christopher Stone demonstrated this oddity, when he opened Harrods' new gramophone salons in April 1929:

"This was... built specially by E.M.G. for the scientific study of records from a phonetic point of view; it is believed to be the only one of its kind in England. The results were extraordinarily interesting. Mr Bernard Shaw's Spoken English Broken English became in reverse, a queer language that was claimed by listeners to resemble Russian, Dutch, even Erse. Cortot's playing of Chopin's 24th Prelude was even more unexpected in its organ like and fantastic behaviour..."

Ginn, as creative a self publicist as ever, allowed himself a little joke in the small ads at the back of *The Gramophone*:

"If the gentleman who stole a de-luxe model of the Wilson Horn model from the E.M.G. showrooms, between 12.30 and 2.30 on Wednesday the 8th May will kindly call again, Mr Ginn will be pleased to present him with a Wilson Horn, and also to tune the soundbox for his exact requirements!"

In the Alice in Wonderland world of eccentricity, another oddity was taking shape. Ginn and Davey had for some time been convinced that with a longer acoustic system they could get even better reproduction. The snag was that a larger horn was needed, but it could not be got into a cabinet without folding it, which they were unwilling to do. The length of system they calculated they would need would preclude the use of a straight horn, for it would have had to be something over six feet long. It was, in the end, Ginn and David Phillips who suggested that it should stand on top of the motor box, and take the question mark shape we are accustomed to today. Once again it was Davey who worked out the mathematics. In the interests of keeping costs to a minimum, the horn was again to be built of layers of laminated paper. Horns of this date have been found to contain the pages of London telephone directories, and daily newspapers.

E.M.G. Prototype Mark X.

This new machine was Davey's Mark X. It was first demonstrated at the Richmond and District gramophone Society as early as March 1929, when it was referred to as the Davey Isophonic Horn machine. It broke new ground in its appearance, the horn being the largest ever fitted to an acoustic machine. Being an even more extraordinary phenomenon than the Wilson Horn model, they must have entertained some doubts as to its acceptability in normal households. Indeed *The Gramophone* dryly observed:

"It is decidedly the connoisseur's gramophone; one can imagine many a housewife being taken aback at the sight of the external horn rising majestically from the back of the cabinet; she may have doubts as to how it will look in the corner of her drawing room; but if she has any music in her soul, she will decide, when she has heard it play, that it must look well. Apodeictic judgements are the privilege of our wives...."

Once the Mark X had been demonstrated at Richmond, news of its performance spread like a bushfire through the gramophone world. Everyone wanted one. The order books were full before it had even got into serious production, and there is some evidence that the strength of the demand caused E.M.G. to hurry it into production before it was really tested properly. No doubt the financial pressures they felt under contributed to the haste, after all it was a new feeling for them to have a debt of £5,000 to service. In fact news of the Mark X's performance had probably been exaggerated, its dramatic presence leading people to believe that it performed as extraordinarily as it appeared. The acoustic system was not much longer than the Wilson Horn model, and to today's ear, the performance was much the same, though with a slightly better bass. The horn, surely the feature which created so much interest, was poorly designed from a structural point of view. The whole weight was borne by the narrow neck, and this was inadequate, causing the great horn to sag before long. With the Mark X came a completely new soundbox, a sophisticated design with an almost infinite capacity for adjustment, and this was as much responsible for the improvements in reproduction as the great horn itself.

The Gramophone gave the Mark X an enthusiastic welcome although there were reservations. "The Mark X model is one that continues in all respects to carry on the policy that gramophone connoisseurs have come to associate with the firm of E.M.G., which is that sound acoustic considerations must take complete precedence in the design. We have therefore a machine which might be described as somewhat freakish in appearance, judged by conventional standards. If you imagine an enthusiastic gramophile fully versed in the acoustical theory of the problem, setting out to design his own gramophone from first principles, he would probably create a machine not unlike the E.M.G. model, except that the Mark X bears no sign of the amateur about its beautiful workmanship...

As regards the performance of the machine, we may say at once that the Mark X, rather as we expected, is certainly right in the front rank. Although we have criticisms to express, these arise in consequence of the very high standard we feel justified in adopting in judging this machine.

The quality of reproduction is so clearly ahead of that of any other commercial instrument at anything like the same price that the only standards of comparison on which we could base a proper appraisement were its predecessor from the same factory and our recollections of original performances. As readers know, we have a very high opinion of the earlier (Wilson Horn) machine, and we must confess that at first we were inclined to doubt whether the Mark X excels it in quite the ratio of the respective prices... A comparison of the two machines reveals that the Mark X has the same clarity and resolving power and general even response of its predecessor, and by virtue of its larger horn, it explores the bass regions more effectively. On the other hand, with fibre needles at any rate, the sound projection seemed a trifle backward, and the extreme treble a little weak..."

Once again, every sinew was at full stretch at Grape Street in an attempt to catch up with orders. The firm was making money now faster than it ever had before. The record department was already beginning, under Balfour Davey's guidance, to acquire a reputation for sound judgement and advice. The range of products was growing. David Phillips was developing new techniques for tuning electrical pick-ups by other makers, and E.M.G. was able to offer for the first time their own pick-up arm, which had about it the look of a design by F.G.G. Davey. Yet all was not well beneath the surface.

It had been at Herbert West's suggestion, even insistence, that Ginn should appoint a business manager to co-ordinate the work of all departments, and supplies of materials to them, so that a smooth flow of machines was achieved. Ginn had taken on a man from his old regiment, the R.A.S.C., called George Green. Green knew all about arranging supplies, as he had been quarter master sergeant in the army, and he had a pretty fair understanding of corporate finance, which made him the only one at Grape Street who had. He was not an easy man to like. His manner was hectoring. He achieved efficiency by bullying, where he might have achieved equal success by diplomacy. Soon enough tensions began to develop between Green and Ginn. Green never regarded Ginn as a proper soldier, as he had not seen action in the war. The fact that Ginn had been commissioned did nothing to smooth out these tensions, indeed, it made them worse. Ginn regarded Green as an 'other rank'. Green on the other hand treated the Daveys with an irritating deference.

These difficulties might have led nowhere, were it not for a seemingly unconnected event. The chaos theory suggests that the flap of the butterfly's wing can bring about a hurricane hundreds of miles away, so perhaps it was the chaos theory that was now operating. Green happened to mention to Ginn one day that he knew of a fine house for sale in the same road that Green lived in. It was a bargain. It was called Cromlech, in Edgwarebury Lane, Edgware. We shall never be sure whether Ginn was actually looking for a house at that time or not, although we do know that Esther Ginn wanted to live away from her mother's dominance. It was true he did by now have a son and daughter, and he might well have thought it was time to take the plunge. He certainly had a thriving business, and a healthy business bank account. Either way, he went to see Cromlech, and later bought it. Why should he not begin to enjoy the fruits of sweet success?

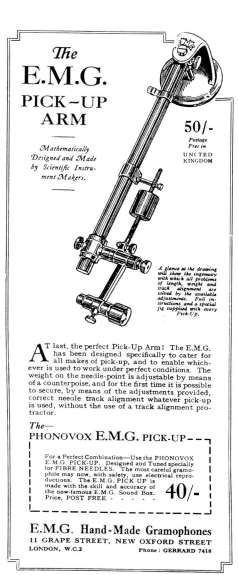

Darrieulat's serpentine chest.

The first mistake he made was buying the house with some of the remaining loan capital. The second was furnishing it. It was now that Ginn's predilection for quality turned out to be disastrous. Another man might have been content to furnish his house with whatever furniture he could beg or borrow. Not so Michael Ginn. He wanted the best that money could buy. He placed an order with Frank Darrieulat that must have made the little Frenchman's eyes bulge. Ginn wanted a birds eye maple dining table of circular design, and large size. He wanted a massive oak sideboard, a lady's bureau, a serpentine chest, a grandmother clock, and there may have been much more besides. It was by any standard a tremendous order. The furniture was not to be of veneered ply, like the gramophone cases, it was to be built of well seasoned oak, with luxurious and exotic veneers over the top.

The sheer size of this commission would have brought production of gramophone cases to an abrupt halt, and therefore all gramophones. This seizure of production brought Ginn into direct conflict with Green. Green remonstrated fiercely, but it made no difference. Ginn took the standpoint that it was his firm, his money, and so he could do as he wished. The trouble was he was wrong on all three counts. The money he had used belonged to the firm. The money had been lent to increase production, and Ginn had brought that to a halt. This had caused profits to fall sharply. As the 25% of the profits which West was charging was based on the profits the company should now be making, as a result of increased production, Ginn had not a leg to stand on, and Green knew it. Ginn told him if he did not like the way he ran the firm, he could go elsewhere. He did. He went straight to see Herbert West.

When Ginn heard what Green had done, he was furious. He saw it as an act of gross disloyalty. He did not improve matters when he invited Green to tea at Cromlech, where Esther Ginn solemnly served him a with a comport full of grass which concealed a snake - well, a slow worm. Green was not in the least amused. Relations between Ginn and his business manager reached an all time low.

This train of events bewildered Ginn, and threw him off balance. He was very angry at Green's disloyalty, but also confused. He was an innocent where finance was concerned, and he had never really grasped the restrictions that borrowing capital would impose on him. In the past he had relied on his wits to get him out of trouble, but this time, no matter what he did, he did not seem able to escape. He felt trapped.

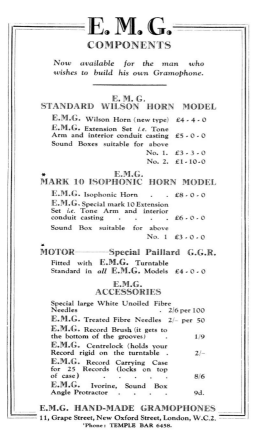
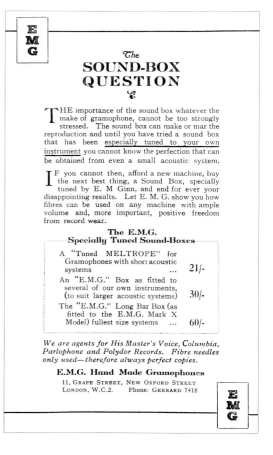

Although his train of thought had started with Green, whom he now regarded as a traitor, his mind turned to other possibilities. He remembered how Green fawned on the Daveys, and this led him to speculate on whether Green was in league with them somehow. There was some hostility developing anyway between Ginn and the Daveys, because Balfour Davey's appointment to the Expert Committee of *The Gramophone*, had elevated him to a plane that was inaccessible to Ginn, which left him feeling a bit out of it. If they were all in league with each other, had he been set up to buy the house, if so why? Was it all a clever scheme to take the firm away from him? This prompted him to question whether Herbert West himself was a part of the plot. Anyone who has ever felt threatened by a conspiracy will know how easily thin evidence can rapidly assume monstrous proportions, how doubt can be transformed into certainty. At the end of that particular route lies paranoia, and Michael Ginn was travelling down it.

His feelings of doubt about the Daveys were compounded by the fact that he knew in his heart of hearts that he had exploited them. Balfour Davey had not been rewarded for his designs other than being allowed the satisfaction of seeing them turned into practical form. The record department depended on his knowledge of serious music for its growing reputation, and the authority of his advice. Frank Davey, though his involvement was relatively small at this stage, was becoming involved in the electrical side of the business. Ginn wanted to expand this, but he recognised that he was likely to become dependent on Frank Davey to carry this out. Again, he felt trapped.

By the time Ginn received the inevitable summons to see Herbert West, he had convinced himself of the existence of a conspiracy against him. He was in no mood to be humble, and he certainly was not going to allow West, whom he now believed to be the ringleader, to lecture him. West, who had vast experience of the world, could not allow Ginn to get away with what really amounted to fraudulent misappropriation of the firm's funds - it might even be embezzlement. It was a bad basis on which the two men met and the meeting resolved nothing. All Ginn heard was that he had accepted the loan to increase production. In his unbalanced state, this sounded to him as though he was being told to go for mass production. This he flatly refused to do. It was an impasse, which left West very seriously concerned about the situation.

Ginn returned to his brooding. He now sought means by which he might regain control of the firm, but he was not thinking straight, which led him to make his last and fatal blunder. He reasoned that if he could only get rid of Green, and the electrical side of the business, he would get rid also of Frank Davey. If there was trouble with Balfour Davey over this, he would get rid of him as well. The firm had already advertised that they were about to offer a new radio gramophone. This was to be built to the recommended design of the Expert Committee, with Frank Davey's supervision of the actual manufacture.

The first phase of the master plan was to abandon the new radio gramophone. Ginn advertised in *The Gramophone* that it was as yet impossible to obtain the same standard of unvarying excellence and reliability from electrical reproducers, as could be got from the acoustic gramophone, so he was abandoning that side of the business. Had he been thinking clearly, he would have realised

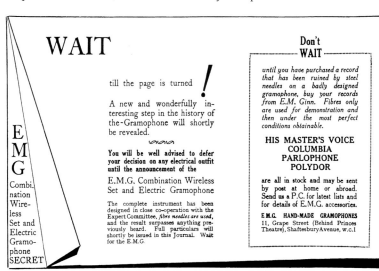

that he would never be allowed to get away with such an outrageous and dishonest claim. He had sown the wind, and would shortly reap the whirlwind.

The world of the gramophone was small and intimate. Balfour Davey was a personal friend of Percy Wilson, and it was inevitable that Ginn's intentions should have been understood, and discussed between the two men. Retribution came swiftly; from Wilson.

"I cannot let pass the statements made in the E.M.G. advertisement last month. I have no doubt they were made in good faith, and that their full import was not realised at the time. I have already admitted as everyone of experience must, that the difficulties of standardising electrical reproducers are considerable. But it is merely foolish to assert so categorically that 'the same standard of excellence and reliability is as yet unobtainable in electric reproducers as in ordinary gramophones.' For you see, I happen to know that Mr Ginn decided to give up the attempt before he really made it. From time to time, Mr Ginn has received a good deal of help from our Expert Committee, and I feel sure he would be the first to admit it."

By now, Ginn had really backed himself into a corner, and it was difficult to see how he could escape. Herbert West was not prepared to allow Ginn to get rid of George Green or Frank Davey, and certainly not Balfour Davey. Percy Wilson was not prepared to allow Ginn to posture about his reasons for abandoning the electrical side of things, to cover his true intentions. Ginn was not so much trying to skate on thin moral ice, as to walk on the water.

Throughout the early autumn of 1929, the business itself continued to expand, now the backlog caused by the furniture order had been passed. Davey's Mark IV table model

An E.M.G. Mark IV.

44

appeared, as a cheap alternative to the more exotic models, and Frank Darrieulat's patented record storage unit was added to the range of quality accessories. This latter allowed records to be stored flat but when the drawers were pulled open, presented the records vertically. The soured relationships at Grape Street were carefully concealed from the eyes of the customers, but they continued to fester, and in time might have resulted on their own in destroying the firm. But there was a further blow that fell. In October the Wall Street Crash sent the world into a financial nose-dive towards depression. It was this factor that forced Herbert West to take steps to secure his investment in E.M.G. What may well have started out as a whimsical investment, now became a matter of deadly earnest.

The E.M.G.
RECORD STORAGE CABINET

has been designed with all the skill, and is made with the same care, which has brought the E.M.G. Hand-made Gramophones to the forefront. It is undoubtedly the ideal Storage Cabinet for the man who cares for his records and who realises what an important part is played by the method of storage in the life of his collection. The E.M.G. Record Storage Cabinet accommodates 128 records in drawers ; each drawer has a separate lock. The records lie flat, immune from warping and divided from each other by plain, non-abrasive cards, which are supplied at no extra cost. This arrangement allows the maximum elasticity from an indexing point of view and any desired system may be used. By means of an ingenious and reliable hinge device the drawers pull out and then swing downwards, presenting the records on edge right in front in the full light, immediately accessible whether the first or last record in the drawer is required. There is no groping or peering in dark recesses with the E.M.G. Cabinet. The top of the cabinet will accommodate the largest E.M.G. Table Gramophone. Several models of this storage cabinet are being made in order to accommodate larger collections and properly to house sets of records in Albums. We invite you to write at once for full particulars.

Dimensions
Height 40"
Width   21½"
Depth   24"

Oak
£12 : 12 : 0
Mahogany or Walnut
£13 : 10 : 0

E.M.G. Hand-made Gramophones Limited
11, GRAPE ST., Shaftesbury Avenue, LONDON, W.C.1 (Phone: TEMPLE BAR 6458)

Herbert West was a very wise man, and when he failed to achieve harmony at Grape Street by persuasion, he knew that he was going to have to impose a solution of his own design. Solomon himself would have been delighted with West's answer. Recognising that the real strength of the firm lay in the hands of the Daveys and not in Ginn's abilities, and that it was Ginn's wild behaviour that needed to be controlled, he devised what looked like an extremely fair solution. He proposed that E.M.G. should be re-constituted as a limited company, controlled by a board of directors, of which he would be chairman. There should be a nominal share capital of £30,000 in £1 shares. The company should purchase E.M.G. for £5,000 (the amount of the original loan). 20,000 shares would be allocated to Ginn, making him the majority shareholder. However, of those 20,000 shares, Ginn would have to allocate 8,250 to West, and a further 2,000 shares to Balfour Davey, 'for services rendered in carrying on the business hitherto, and for continuing to render similar services after the formation of the company.' In addition Ginn had to pay West the sum of £750 in cash. It was a masterly arrangement, and ultimately a just one, though Ginn did not agree. He was still the majority shareholder, which went some way to preserving his dignity and status in the firm, but now he could be out-voted by an alliance of West and Davey. Ginn had lost control of E.M.G., but Davey had at long last received some reward and recognition. The new company was registered on December 30th, 1929.

Looking backwards down the tunnel of the years, this was a tragedy that need never have happened. The cause of all the trouble had been Ginn's ignorance of the financial facts of life, coupled with his subsequent refusal to acknowledge his mistake. The irony was that in the first six months of trading at Grape Street the firm had made a net profit of almost £1,900, showing that there would have been plenty of scope to offer either one or both the Daveys a partnership. Sadly, too much venom had already been injected, too many hard words spoken, for the new arrangement to have had much chance of working. Ginn still chose to regard the new situation as the result of a deliberate conspiracy to steal his firm from him. It would have been surprising indeed if he had been able to work with colleagues he regarded as spies and traitors, and so it turned out. The few board meetings that were called were increasingly acrimonious, and the end came in March 1930, when Ginn gave them all the benefit of his opinions on their ancestry, its legality, and their business ethics. All his frustrations of the previous months were released in one poisonous blast of bitterness, after which he resigned from the board, and left the premises.

Turning his back on Grape Street he spent many hours wandering the streets of London, trying to come to terms with what had befallen him, and the injustice of it. When finally he returned to "Cromlech" exhausted, defeated and depressed beyond measure, what must he have felt, as he surveyed his sumptuously furnished home?

Davey Radiogram DR5.

Chapter Four

The Horn Wars

The customer visiting Grape Street in April 1930 would have noticed little to indicate the constitutional earthquake that had struck E.M.G.. The club atmosphere persisted. A sense of unruffled calm pervaded the building. Balfour Davey was now managing director, and occupied what had been Ginn's office on the first floor. Davey had felt obliged to resign from the Expert Committee, to avoid any suggestions of commercial bias.

The Gramophone rather coyly reported:
"The large showroom recently opened in the basement of 11, Grape Street, at last gives visitors a chance of hearing all the E.M.G. models in surroundings approximating to home conditions, instead of being cooped up in an audition room and flattered by a 'beau fibreur' of a salesman under the shadow of a Mark X horn, the size of a liner's ventilator."

This report concealed from the public the fact that the basement was only vacant because Horace Hill had moved out. As Ginn's personal friend, he had watched aghast as the pageant played itself out. He had been most unhappy about his position, and had decided to pull out and set up business elsewhere. He took premises near to Great Ormond Street. He retained E.M.G.'s business, but now on a more independent basis. The sly reference to a 'beau fibreur of a salesman' was clearly a swipe at Ginn. There were those on *The Gramophone* staff who were going to find it hard to forgive Ginn for the way he had behaved.

Whereas Ginn's vision of E.M.G. had been focused on selling things to gramophiles, Balfour Davey's was more to do with the provision of a complete service for music lovers. Some idea of how he wanted the record department to serve the public can be gleaned from an E.M.G. advertisement in *The Gramophone* in May 1930:
"A new and better way to buy your records is offered by E.M.G.

When do you get your best ideas about records to buy? Is it when you visit a gramophone shop, possibly after a tiring day? There are distractions in the shop too. You probably hear the new month's issues being played; perhaps you like and buy one or two. But were they the records that best satisfied your own individual taste, or best filled the gaps in your own collection? Probably not; yet the records you really want are so much more precious to you than those you just like a bit when you hear them played. You probably get your best ideas when playing your own machine at home, or at a concert, or simply when thinking about music in a quiet moment.

For you then, the E.M.G. plan has been devised. whenever you get an idea about records ring up E.M.G. on the spur of the moment. Ask for 'Records', give your name and say what interested you. Your name will be entered in a book, and under it will be written what work, composer or performer has aroused your interest. Searches of catalogues will be made, and the results entered up. When you visit E.M.G. a few days weeks or months later, you need remember nothing but your own name. Give this, and your own personal interests will at once be recalled to you, questions will be readily answered, and the records indicated will await your judgement. The advice of an expert and music lover will be at your service..."

The customer, when he called at Grape Street and made himself known, would be quietly ushered into an audition room. Here the record would be placed on a turntable. He would be politely asked if he understood how to cut the fibre needles, and if he did, the soundbox would be placed on the record and he would be left alone to enjoy it. There was never the slightest hint of pressure to buy. E.M.G. existed only to provide a first class service, the atmosphere Davey wanted was not that usually found in a shop, but that found in exclusive clubs. Many people entering Grape Street for the first time, who lacked confidence, or felt touchy about their musical ignorance, were very often put off by this slightly superior atmosphere, and left, never to return. The serious music lover stayed, and returned ever after, and he was the customer Davey wanted. The service was extended in 1930 by the publication of the *Monthly Letter*, which listed for E.M.G. customers the latest worthwhile issues from all the major record companies, marked for interpretation and recording quality by Balfour Davey and Tom Fenton. This *Monthly Letter* was sent to all customers who wanted it, and it kept them in touch with Grape Street ensuring that they ordered their records by post if they could not attend the shop in person. This letter was posted to all parts of the world, and the assured quality of judgement on the records, soon built for E.M.G. a reputation which could not be approached by any other record business in Britain. Finally, E.M.G. also issued their *Foreign List* of worthwhile records culled from the foreign lists of the major companies.

Between March and May 1930, lawyers for Ginn and West fought out the final details of the separation of Ginn from E.M.G. Ginn's resignation had caused all sorts of problems. The biggest and most pressing question was the name of the firm. This was clearly associated in the public mind with Ginn himself. R.H. Behrend and Co., West's lawyers who had drafted the constitution of the new company, argued that the name of the company was part of the equity the company had bought from Ginn. Ginn's lawyer, who was just a customer of Ginn's who happened to be a lawyer, as opposed to Behrend and Co., who were experts in company legislation, counter argued that it was not possible to prevent a man from trading in his own name. Then there was the question of the shares. Ginn was still the majority shareholder in E.M.G., though no longer a director. This was a situation that could not be allowed to continue. Agreement was eventually reached for the company to buy Ginn's shares, in exchange for the right to leave the company's name unchanged. An attempt was made to get Ginn to agree not to re-enter the gramophone business, either in his own name or any other. This was resisted. At the beginning of the negotiations, Ginn was not too worried about this condition, because he had rather lost interest in the gramophone business, but as the weeks dragged by, he began to dig his feet in. Behrend and Co., had to yield on these points, and Ginn was not prohibited from starting again in his own name, though he was forbidden to use the letters E.M.G. The threat of what would happen to him if he attempted to break this condition was to leave him permanently unsure of exactly what he was allowed to do, and nervous about using even his own name. The final detail that had to be attended to was Ginn's replacement on the board, and his place was filled by Herbert West's son, H.H. West.

H.M. Bateman's sketch of the Wests on a day on the "Kathleen" in 1928. H.H. West on extreme left and H.E. West on extreme right.

While these tortuous negotiations were proceeding, Ginn was by no means sure of his future. He was bitterly despondent disillusioned, and still bewildered. The speed with which calamity had overtaken him made this hardly surprising. He thought it most unlikely that he would be able to start up in competition with E.M.G. The connoisseur's market was a small one, and the niche was adequately filled by E.M.G. Any firm trying to set up in competition would find it a formidable task. E.M.G. was now properly capitalised and well organised, and its reputation second to none.

As his thoughts began to clear, and his initial rage at his perceived injustice began to subside, he began to hear what his friend E.J. Creese had been saying to him for weeks. Creese argued that Ginn's best asset was his name, which was highly thought of in the gramophone world. As he was still allowed to use it, Why not? Creese used many compelling arguments why Ginn should not lie down and give up, but it was not until he pointed out another aspect, that his arguments began to tell on Ginn. Creese cunningly agreed that the market place was small and exclusive, but that if Ginn re-entered it every machine he sold would be a sale that was denied to E.M.G. This fact had not occurred to Ginn. If he started again, surely David Phillips would come with him? The idea that he might be able to re-create the old geometry of the Holborn days, when it was just family, began to seem quite attractive. The idea that he might be able to exert a slow and strangulating pressure on E.M.G. had even greater attractions, and from the tone of his later advertising, it really seems as though revenge was the greater motive, building the very best machine came second.

It was typical of Ginn that once his mind was made up, he allowed nothing to get in the way. He sold his house, and moved back to the Phillips's house at Ingerthorpe in Highgate. This was a large Edwardian house owned by the Church Commissioners, but leased to Joe Phillips. There were plenty of large rooms and the Ginns were warmly welcomed back. In May 1930, Ginn had his first success. He took the grim satisfaction of poaching David Phillips from E.M.G.

By one of those fortunate coincidences, about a year earlier, Ginn had discussed with Percy Wilson how E.M.G. might be able further to improve the Mark X's acoustic system. Wilson had advised that the only way would be to try to reduce the number of bends. He had even suggested a shape of horn that would achieve this. They had discussed the shape of the U tube, which in the Mark X had some very sharp bends in it. So, when they came to designing the new range of machines, they merely adopted the Wilson suggestions of the previous year. Joe Ginn can remember his father and uncle laying out sheets of lining paper on his bedroom floor, so they could plot the shape of the new horns.

Designing the soundboxes was also straightforward. The E.M.G. box was derived from the research of all the amateur soundbox designers whose best ideas Percy Wilson had concentrated into its present E.M.G. form. It is true that Dave Phillips did a great deal of experimenting with this basic design, and became the master of soundbox tuning, but the design was Wilson's. This left E.M.G. unable to protect their soundbox by patent. Hence, it was a simple matter for Phillips to imitate the principle, making only minor alterations. While the men were engaged in designing the new range, Esther Ginn started making fibre needles by the thousand.

When it came to thinking of a new name for their enterprise, the choice of Expert surely was a tilt at *The Gramophone*, seeking to associate Ginn's product in the public mind with the Expert Committee. This implied a spurious seal of approval from what amounted to *The Gramophone's* governing body. It was a clever jest and nothing was done to challenge the name, because nothing could be done.

While Ginn made clear in his every utterance exactly how bitter he felt, the Daveys kept their silence. This silence concealed an almost equal feeling of dismay at the way things had turned out. Frank Davey, many years later let slip that he thought Ginn had let him and his brother down very badly, financially. This is the only evidence of their feelings, but their dismay is completely understandable. Prior to the Great Schism, whatever financial arrangements they had supposed to exist, had clearly failed. After the split, they were left with a company which was under the control of the Wests, who had financed it. There were demands for increased production and further expansion of business, with a view to increasing profits. These commercial pressures acted directly against Balfour Davey's vision of what E.M.G. should be, making further conflict probable. These differences of perspective might have proved an insuperable obstacle to a lesser man than Herbert West. He realised in time, that Davey's vision of providing an excellent service to the serious music lover at the lowest cost might well in the long run, still result in a first class business. As they came to see this happening in practice, the Wests made it clear that they wished to exercise no further personal role in the running of the company.

In fact relations between Balfour Davey and H.H. West remained cordial for the whole of the next forty years. H.H. West can remember Davey telephoning him one day and enquiring if he would like a flight in an aeroplane. He had not flown before, but he accepted the invitation. They went to Hanger Lane, where there was a bi-plane belonging to a friend of Davey's. Davey inspected it, and took it up for a few circuits to make sure everything was working well. Then he picked up the young West and they flew to Fareham in Hampshire to visit a friend of Davey's. After coffee, they flew on to Wiltshire for lunch with another of Davey's friends. After lunch they went on again to visit a farmer friend, where they had to make a number of low passes over the field in front of the house to clear the cattle from their intended runway. It was a trip that West was never to forget. He said of Balfour Davey "He was as good a scientist as he was a pilot, and he was an excellent pilot."

Perhaps where the Daveys felt cheated the worst, was Ginn's starting again in the gramophone business. The niche market that E.M.G. commanded at the time of the split, was big enough for one comfortably, but not for two. Ginn's restart put an unlooked for pressure on E.M.G., and really did deprive them of a significant amount of business over the years.

In June 1930, Expert Handmade Gramophones opened their first London showroom, just off Oxford Street, at 55, Rathbone Place. In the same month, manufacture of the Mark X at Grape Street had at last caught up with orders, and even soundboxes could be supplied within three days of order. E.M.G.'s June advertisement in *The Gramophone* set out the firm's extensive stall. It showed a range of goods and services to the gramophile that was impressively comprehensive, and for the first time allowed Balfour Davey to claim the credit for the designs of all current E.M.G. models.

This advertisement, showing the full extent of the E.M.G. range of goods and services in all its glory, and seeming to claim for Davey all the credit, was too much for Ginn to stomach. In a following advertisement he gave vent to a splenetic outburst:

"We take pride," he wrote "in advertising our products, not ourselves or our past achievements in the progress of gramophone design - although we have been greatly pressed to do so..." June 1930 then, saw E.M.G. straddling and commanding the market place for the gramophone connoisseur, while precariously perched on the edge of that market place was Expert Gramophones at Rathbone Place. The 'horn wars' had begun.

Chapter Five

Precarious Finances

Ginn's bitterness of heart led him to wage war on Grape Street - a war that seemed at times to be of more importance than the business of making gramophones. It was a war of attrition. Everything Ginn did he did with one eye on Grape Street. In the advertising columns of *The Gramophone* he kept up a continual bombardment of innuendo and invective, verging at times on the truculent, and this barrage was to continue for some years. These literary arrows of resentment rained down on Grape Street, where they were met with, on the whole, a dignified silence.

E.M.G. could afford to ignore them. The Expert range grew steadily, as much to compete with E.M.G. as to provide a first class service to Expert customers. Each item was carefully priced to undercut E.M.G. - the E.M.G. needle cutter cost five shillings, the Expert cutter four shillings, the E.M.G. needle containers cost five shillings and there were no prizes for guessing how much the Expert equivalent cost. This was a price war which did little to harm E.M.G., much to disadvantage Ginn, but it had the dubious benefit of making him feel that his policy of slow revenge was going to be effective.

By July, the first Expert Senior machine was ready for inspection - a tremendous feat of organisation, considering that the whole machine had to be designed from scratch, patterns and moulds made, tooling and a new cabinet maker had to be found, not to mention a new firm found to make the new horns. To begin with, the Expert range of machines was housed in identical boxes, a design forced on Ginn by cost considerations. The boxes were solidly made with veneer finishes, but plain veneer, with a cellulose sprayed finish. They housed acoustic systems of differing length, to which horns of different sizes were added. This was a clever, if necessitous design, but the finished article had a functional appearance, which did not compare favourably with the E.M.G. models which were all French polished, with ebony stringing, and elaborate quartered veneering. Both firms offered a variety of paper finishes for the horns, though E.M.G. offered the greater range of choices.

55 Rathbone Place.

E.M. Ginn's Expert Senior.

The Expert Minor.

Ginn was only too painfully aware that the success of the Expert Senior would be dependent on the opinion of the Expert Committee; this was the Rubicon that must be crossed if he was to be taken seriously again as a maker of connoisseur instruments. Yet he must have feared that this would give the committee the chance they might have been waiting for to revenge themselves on him, for the way he had behaved towards Balfour Davey. When he invited them to inspect the first model, he must have had his heart in his mouth. He need not have feared, for as usual, Percy Wilson was scrupulously fair in his reporting the committee's judgement:

"Then too, there is Mr Ginn's latest gramophone. The committee heard the first model a month ago, and was quite put out of sympathy with electrical reproducers for a while... At Mr Ginn's request, they are deferring a full dress report until further samples of the same model are available, and full experience has been gained in tuning it to concert pitch. In the meantime, there can be little doubt that the committee's considered verdict will be one of unqualified approval. Mr Ginn makes me eat some of my past words, but as he has paid me the compliment of incorporating in this marvel of his a number of suggestions I made to him a year or more ago, I did not expect to suffer from indigestion.'

Bridges had indeed been repaired completely.

It was one thing to bring the Expert Senior to the market place, but quite another to sell it in any numbers. E.M.G. still dominated the market and most national music critics owned Mark Xs. It was hard to see how to break this mould. In the past Ginn had tried to find national figures of note to endorse his machines, to impress potential buyers, and lead them to his door. In this he had been almost too successful, for now he was obliged to seek endorsement from a lesser level of musical notables. The first to oblige him was Professor Kaikhosru Sorabji, a prolific if eccentric composer.

"From time to time during the last few years, I have referred in terms of very high praise to the remarkable gramophones produced by Mr E.M. Ginn. I have recently heard his latest achievement, the Expert as he calls it, and have no hesitation in saying that not only is the instrument not equalled, it is not approached by anything else on the market at the present time. I advise anyone contemplating the purchase of a gramophone to hear Mr Ginn's instrument first and last..." To which Ginn added a footnote that Professor Sorabji had now bought an Expert Senior.

In September 1930, the Expert Junior appeared, followed in December by the Expert Minor which for the time being completed the Expert range of machines, and put Ginn fully into competition with E.M.G.'s acoustic range. It would be true to say that by December 1930 only six months after Ginn had started his new venture, E.M.G. and Expert had firmly locked horns.

The appearance of the Expert range produced a strange anomaly in the specialist gramophone market. While E.M.G. were vastly in control of that market, with their comprehensive service and first class machinery, Expert, though small and struggling, at this time, made better gramophones. Their acoustic systems were superior to the Mark X, and they had better soundboxes. This situation could not be allowed to continue, and Balfour Davey was obliged to try to improve the Mark X. Though when it had first appeared it had broken new ground, establishing for the first time that monstrous external horns could be acceptable in the cause of true reproduction, it did have several faults. The worst of these was the structural instability of the horn. The acoustic system as well, was only marginally longer than the Wilson Horn model. These defects were addressed in the Mark Xa which appeared first in November 1930.

This model had an improved design of tone arm, by courtesy of Percy Wilson, a horn of greater size, supported by an aluminium elbow to carry its weight, and a new soundbox. The acoustic system was lengthened too, which brought it into serious contention with the Expert Senior. When a month later, in December, the Expert Committee got round to reviewing fully the Expert Senior, Balfour Davey must have wondered just what he had to do to retain his former ascendancy, for the article began:

"It is difficult to know what to say about this instrument, save that one can hardly conceive that a much better reproduction will ever be achieved from an acoustic gramophone.."

Neither was there much consolation for Davey when the two machines were compared by *The Gramophone* side by side:

"Our previous hesitation in trying from memory to make any detailed comparison between the two was soon justified. On certain records, particularly those of a year or so ago, we defy even the most critical listener to differentiate between the two models in our office. But there are differences, and very appreciable ones.. as certain other records demonstrated. And some of these differences were contrary to our expectations. Thus we found that the Expert gave a more open quality and more bite on the top strings, and the same sort of effect

 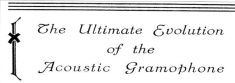

was noticed later in the high vocal passages of an Elisabeth Schumann record. On the other hand, the trombone crescendo about half an inch through the first side of the recent Columbia Funeral March record was beautifully clear and distinct on the Xa, but was rather subdued on the Expert. On the whole, our judgement is that which we have indicated earlier the Xa takes care of individual timbre even to the point of excess at times, while the Expert concentrates rather on a bolder and more forward tone with individual musical qualities sufficiently accurately portrayed to give a realistic blend. The quality of both is clean, clear and detailed..."

The constraints which Balfour Davey's gentlemanliness imposed upon him, his natural reserve, and his total abhorrence of any act of self publicity, were constraints that did not impinge upon Michael Ginn, in the least. To him, any method which sold machines was permissible, even though some of his sales methods embarrassed David Phillips. Whilst Davey would not have dreamed of breaking the confidence of his noble clients by using their names and titles for his own benefit, Ginn felt no such compunction. Soon his advertisements began to convey the impression that Expert gramophones was a subsidiary of Debrett. Lady Beatrice Thynne, the Countess of Rosebery and Lord Berners were the first titled people to buy Expert machines, and Ginn shamelessly used their names, as he was to do with every other titled customer as the years rolled by. It was clever ground on which to do battle, for he knew that Davey would not deign to compete.

Even in the small advertisements at the very back of *The Gramophone*, Ginn never missed an opportunity of needling E.M.G. There appeared such malicious little gems as:

"E.M.G. Mark X for sale - owner buying Expert. Apply 55, Rathbone Place." and:

"E.M.G. Mark Xa for sale in perfect condition - can be had of E.M. Ginn, Rathbone Place."

This latter advertisement arose from an amusing circumstance that Ginn was able to turn to his own advantage. He received one day, a telephone call from the principal of a grand private school in Highgate. It was a sad story. They had bought an E.M.G. Xa from Grape Street, and had set it up in the gymnasium. At first it had performed well, but after a time, its voice gradually sank to a muffled whisper. They called in E.M.G., who came and took it away. It was set up again by the men from Grape Street, who offered no explanation of what had been wrong with it. When for the second time it lost its voice, the principal of the school got in touch with Ginn.

An "Expert" Profile

A glance at the various details will at once show, not only why the "Expert" is the most successful machine of to-day, but also how it differs in fundamental design from all other gramophones

MASTER PATENT No. 18771/30

The "Expert" horn Removable in one second. Totally unaffected by climatic conditions. The longest Acoustic System ever fitted to any exterior horn gramophone.

Note Steel rim built up inside horn material for extra strength.

Special Spring Steel support built into horn material.

Note that the lid is not cut; this also makes for greater strength

Note Special Handmade cabinet-work. Pedestal model cabinets in any wood or design to order.

The "Expert" horn The Logarithmic or Exponential calculations of all "Expert" horns are accurate to ·001 degree.

"Expert" horns can now be supplied in any Colour or Shade to match any furnishing scheme.

Make special note of absence of undesirable bends here.

When used as a Radio Loud Speaker the "Expert" Moving Coil Unit fits here.

Note large diameter here, over twice that of any other machine.

Note enormous strength of construction; the Conduit is bolted right through the cabinet.

Note distance between tone-arm bend and horn bend, actually three times greater than any other exterior horn gramophone.

Every "Expert" model, the Senior at £32 10 0, the Junior at £22 10 0 and the Minor at £17 10 0, is exactly the same in Design, Construction, and Materials; all are Handmade throughout (except the motor) and just as much trouble is taken to thoroughly satisfy the purchaser of an Expert Minor as the purchaser of an Expert Senior

E M Ginn

55 Rathbone Place, Oxford Street, W.1

Ginn knew perfectly well that the only reason an acoustic gramophone can lose its voice is due to some obstruction in the system. With his unerring sense of how to sell, he obligingly sent David Phillips to the school equipped with an Expert Senior, which he installed in the gymnasium, removing the Xa for examination. The very next morning, Ginn rang the principal to ask how the Expert Senior was performing. The school was delighted with it. Ginn suggested that as it had a ten year guarantee, the school might like to buy, and he would allow them a couple of pounds for the Xa. To this they agreed. What they did not know was that when David Phillips had got the Xa back to Rathbone Place, he had merely taken off the horn, and soundbox, and had blown down the tonearm. This had produced a pretty fountain of ping pong balls from where the horn had been! It would have been a week or so before the school would have realised that it had been 'had'. These tactics made David Phillips squirm with embarrassment.

[These large open horned machines so admired by their devoted owners (and so despised by the mass manufacturers like E.M.I. who regarded them as plainly ridiculous) retained their dignity only so long as they remained in their owners homes. Once they were taken from their customary environment, they attracted mirth and ridicule, and on occasion were known to have caused a sensation. One proud owner, moving house in the 1930s, refused to entrust his machine to the removal firm, but took it with him on the train. When he arrived at Waterloo, he called a couple of porters. One carried the motor box, he carried his suitcases, and the second porter brought up the rear carrying the horn under his arm, making station announcements down it to the astonishment of other passengers. Another Mark X owner coming down from Cambridge in his small car at the end of one term, was forced to put the horn on the roofrack, as it would not fit into the car. As he was nearing home, travelling down a country lane, he was horrified to hear the sound of the horn falling off the roof onto the road. As he reversed frantically back up the road, he saw to his horror a lorry fast approaching the defenceless horn. Its wheels were locked, and smoke billowed from the tyres. Both vehicles ended up inches from the horn on either side of it. The lorry driver slowly descended from his cab, took off his cap and scratched his head, uttering the immortal words: "Well then; what kind of snail do you call *that* then?" Another Mark X (Why was it that funny things never seemed to happen to Expert Seniors?) travelled all the way to Australia. Once the queen of the ballroom of the Imperial Hotel at Torquay, it was retained by its owner more for its dramatic appearance than for its voice, which was thin and muffled. After years of dissatisfaction with its performance, an examination was finally made of its tubes, and stuck firmly down the horn, out of sight was found - a teddy bear.

Perhaps the best horn story of all was to do with a man who used to entertain his local gramophone society by taking along his Mark X, in two journeys - one for the box, and one for the horn. So in the early evening, he would solemnly carry the machine in its two parts to the premises where the society met. When the meeting had finished, usually about ten thirty or so, he would carry the box home, then return for the horn. It was his custom to carry the horn over his shoulder, with the bell facing backwards. He often used to wonder why on occasions, as he passed the public house on his way home some men seemed to take one look at him and bolt back inside. It was years later that he discovered that several customers who had taken more than was good for them had reported that as they had come out of the public house, they had seen an elephant in the street!]

The first two years of the 1930s were very difficult ones for all businesses, and the gramophone business was no exception. Many firms disappeared and of these perhaps Orchosol was the most regrettable. Like E.M.G. the firm had accepted inward investment and had become a limited company, but attempts to capitalise on the reputation of these superb machines failed, and the company vanished like so many others into financial limbo. It is though an ill wind that blows no-one any wood, and from this wreck E.M.G. was able to recruit Reggie Brayne, as their business and advertising manager. He had been with Orchosol through its golden years, since 1923, and he had a thorough understanding of all aspects of the gramophone business. One of his first innovations was the inauguration of the Mark Xa club. Membership of this club, at the sum of a mere half-crown a year, entitled attendance at Grape Street in the evenings after work, where concerts of the latest records were given on the first floor. Every imaginable way had to be tried that might result in a sale of anything. Ginn, always with one eye on E.M.G, responded by inviting customers to Rathbone Place in the evenings to hear the symphony concerts on Expert Radio. E.M.G. offered painted horns for the first time, Ginn responded by offering horns painted in any one of sixty colours, or even wood grained finish. So the horn wars continued.

Whereas E.M.G. tended to attract the more sedate and serious type of customer, Ginn revelled in the eccentric, as he had always done - C.K. Ogden being the first. It may have been because Ginn was slightly larger than life himself; or it may be because he had the showman's blood running in his veins. He could number amongst his ancestors Mat Wells, the famous bare knuckle boxer, as well as a number of music hall performers. In his generation, Leslie Henson was a relation too. Ginn had also been a close friend of the Chaplins, Charlie and Syd, indeed he had almost gone to America to work with Syd as a cameraman's assistant.

The Mark Xa in the panelled room at Grape Street.

Perhaps too, the slightly superior atmosphere at Grape Street was too much for the eccentric to stomach, and so they preferred to do business with Michael Ginn at Rathbone Place. This slightly surreal society turned out to be a rich seam to mine, for each eccentric seemed to have connections with others in the musical, literary or artistic world.

Lord Berners is a good example. His appearance, short, squat and hairy, simian his friends called it, together with his wide eyed and innocent expression deceived the unwary completely. He was a great favourite at dinner parties where his cultured wit and charm disarmed people especially the ladies. It was his custom to beg the most beautiful ladies for their photographs, and to continue to plead until their modesty was finally overcome, and they agreed. He was far too much of a gentleman to explain exactly why he required the likenesses. At home, he was compiling, to the accompaniment of shrieks of laughter, the Berners Book of Beauties, where page followed page of the beauties of the day, suitably adorned with warts, spectacles, moustaches and blacked out teeth!

Then again, not many lords would have thought of installing a miniature piano in the back of their Rolls Royce. Those who did not know him well, assumed that this was fitted so that on the long chauffeur driven journeys to his house in Italy, he could compose serenely in the back. Not so, for they had not noticed his other piece of equipment. On the back seat there lay a hideous cretinoid mask on a stick. As dusk fell over the Italian countryside, peasants returning from the fields would first hear music playing, wild mad music. Then as the Rolls swept by they would see the cretin face leering at them from the window, before the Rolls disappeared into the darkness.

Leaving his eccentricity to one side, Lord Berner's life was but one thread in the tapestry of British music, art and literature. He was himself an artist, a writer and composer. In 1926, when Diaghilev brought to London his Ballets Russes, Berners received a commission from Diaghilev to write a ballet. The ballet that Berners subsequently composed was based on a book by Sacheverell Sitwell. The collaboration between Sitwell and Berners resulted in Sitwell becoming a client of Ginn's by personal recommendation. This was a method of business which was known to work well, particularly amongst the upper strata of society. Edwin Lutyens for example had built up his architectural practice by this means before the Great War.

When Sacheverell Sitwell joined the ranks of Expert owners in June 1932, Ginn must have rubbed his hands in glee, for his endorsement would be first class publicity. Anything the Sitwells touched attracted it. There was however, a price to pay for this patronage, as he was to discover. The machine had hardly been delivered and set up before postcards began to arrive at Rathbone Place: 'Send a man to oil my gramophone,' one of them read. 'Send a man to tune my soundbox' read another. David Phillips or Edward Creese would then have to be despatched to Weston Hall, Towcester to oblige. In due course this became a nuisance which Ginn thought to try to alleviate. He wrote to Sitwell suggesting that if he would just take a screwdriver and unscrew four screws on the motor board, he could oil his own gramophone. The reply when it came was swift, 'What is a screwdriver?' Ginn knew when he was beaten, and after that all requests for service were met with resigned good humour.

Osbert and Sacheverell Sitwell at their Chelsea flat. These photographs taken by Barbara Ker-Seymer are actually posed to show the Sitwells listening to their Expert. However, on the day the photograph was to be taken, the Expert broke down unaccountably, and they were actually listening to a musical box.

David Phillips found visits to Weston Hall something of an eye opener:
"The whole place was choc-a-bloc with records, all beautifully filed. As you opened the doors of the cabinets the lists of records faced you, all beautifully done - and in the corner behind the machine there was a pile of broken records, really a pile. You can visualise what happened. He (Sitwell) would put on one of the records, to try it, and if he did not like it, he

would hurl it into the corner, and if he did like it, it would be carefully filed. I've never seen such a pile of broken records."

Ginn's willingness to give this highly personal and patient service in the end paid off, as he had always thought it would. Osbert and Sacheverell Sitwell wrote an article in *Harper's Bazaar* entitled, 'We are hopeless gramophonists,' which ended with:

"Finally, which is the best gramophone? There is no best but perhaps the most satisfactory, and the least expensive, is the handmade one constructed by Mr Ginn of Rathbone Place. This is equipped with a huge papier-maché horn, but the ugliness of it has gone the moment the machine plays, and its usefulness in reproduction is apparent. The E.M.G. (sic) is hand wound, which is a drawback to people who are used to an electrically driven engine, but it is arguable that this is never so satisfactory for it causes the tone to fluctuate and moreover buzzes as if a bluebottle were in the room..."

Still the market remained flat and both firms continued to feel the pinch. Things were so bad towards the end of 1931 that Balfour Davey was obliged to reduce the prices of both the big Mark VII and the Wilson Horn model, and in 1932 to introduce a new cheaper intermediate model, the Mark IX, at sixteen guineas. This model, although it was first introduced because Mark Xs were proving more than customers were able to pay, over the years became the most numerous of all the E.M.G. acoustic models and soon replaced the Mark VIII altogether. In the seemingly endless depression, it was the Mark IV table model at twelve guineas and the Mark IX which found the readier market. Some indication of just how hard things were at Grape Street can be gained from the number of conversions of customers' own cabinet machines of other makes that E.M.G. undertook. This business had to be really worked for and it was vital to get it, if the workshops were to be kept open. For many customers it was the only way they could get an E.M.G. acoustic system, but it did result in

E.M.G. Mark IX 1932.

60

some extraordinary looking hybrid machines. The vortex of depression caused yet more desperate measures. Balfour Davey was forced to allow Keith Prowse, who already used a row of Mark Xas for record demonstration purposes to become agent for E.M.G. machines selling them on commission. Ginn did not miss this, and was quick to point out in his next advertisement that, "We are not a company, and we do not allow others to act as our agents..." If it had not been for their record sales, E.M.G. might well have followed Orchosol into financial oblivion.

Ginn who had neither the facility to convert customers' cabinets, nor record sales, was being pushed further and further towards the edge. Where records saved E.M.G., soundboxes and fibre needles saved Ginn. In his first year of trading he sold 147 machines, in his second, only 125. At this level of business, he was on the breadline.

A fresh lease of life for old cabinet gramophones

There are many fine old gramophones with cabinets built to stand a lifetime's wear, built as few are built to-day, but they now stand idle, their acoustic systems being out of date. Their market value, whether given in part exchange or for cash, is practically nil. We offer a means of bringing them into use again by substituting for the old the latest and finest acoustic systems as used in our own machines.

Such "conversions" as we call them—and we have done many—offer several advantages, the first of course being the same fine reproduction as from our hand-made gramophones. Secondly, there is a saving in price when compared with buying a complete instrument; and thirdly, it is usually possible to build in a record cupboard into the bottom of the cabinet in place of the old horn.

A considerable saving in cost

•

The same fine quality of reproduction

The cost of each conversion varies a little with the amount of work involved, but approximate costs are Mark IX £13 10s., Mark Xa £16, Mark XB £20.

A Salon Decca converted to E.M.G. Xb.

61

Chapter Six

A Question of Policy

Desperate times breed desperate measures. Both firms looked for new ways to expand their range of products. Here, as ever, E.M.G. had not one advantage, but two. They still had access to the Expert Committee, and they were able to make use of this committee's electrical and radio contractor, F.E. Godfrey. At first their policy on radio was to stock those items which the Expert Committee recommended, and radios made by Godfrey. They became sole London agents for the Electrogram loud speakers and they stocked the Meltrope pick-up. In 1931, Frank Davey began to design equipment specially for E.M.G. to assemble and sell. First came a local station receiver, the DR1, specially, perhaps uniquely, designed for the quality reproduction of broadcast music. Shortly afterwards, a long distance receiver was added to the range - the DR2. Frank Davey was a true boffin - quiet and uncommunicative - and he was christened by a friend 'the amiable ice-berg.' He was more often than not to be found lost in thought behind a thick haze of pipe smoke. Even his inscrutable features might have allowed a small show of pleasure when he read a generous review of the DR1 by *The Gramophone*:

"Excellent reproduction is available... indeed we have seldom if ever heard better." This gave weight to E.M.G.'s own claim that "The quality of its reproduction is unapproachable. Musical quality has been our first and definite aim - and we have succeeded."

Both models could be used in conjunction with a pick-up and turntable to make a radio-gramophone. For this combination Frank Davey designed a pick-up, the DP1 specially for fibre needles - true to the E.M.G. tradition. The addition of the radio gramophone proved to have benefits not originally thought of. Customers who bought these machines tended to be those who were prepared to put their faith in the latest technology, and this meant that they were most likely to have Mark Xs to part exchange. These acoustic machines could then be re-sold second-hand, or cannibalised for their acoustic systems to fit into other customers' cabinets.

Customers were encouraged to visit Grape Street to watch machines of all types being made. The tours were conducted personally by whichever Davey happened to be available. Here were proudly displayed not just the standard machines, but also the special installations built for public buildings, churches, schools, theatres, even one vast unit built to the order of an aeroplane firm at Heston, which wanted a gramophone and public address system with a range of at least a quarter of a mile.

Michael Ginn could do little more at first than look enviously at the wireless equipment emanating from E.M.G., and regret continually that he had for the moment lost the easy access to the deliberations of the Expert Committee. He and Phillips had virtually no knowledge of the workings of radio, so they were obliged to start from the very beginning if they were to compete with Grape Street. David Phillips bought himself a series of little booklets called 'Wireless Library for the man in the street' by Ralph Stranger, while Ginn cast about for a source of supply. He bought the cabinets for the Expert acoustic machines from Mr Edwards of the City Accumulator Company. This firm also made radios, so it seemed convenient to buy the components for these from Edwards, for Phillips and Creese to assemble at Rathbone Place. These units turned out to be unreliable, either due to poor components, or poor assembly, and initial experiments were not blessed with success. Expert Radio did not acquire a reputation for high quality or reliability. This was partly due to the fact that Ginn was obliged to get his technical information from those on the lower slopes of Olympus, and because of his ignorance, he was at the mercy of the unscrupulous, as well as those who were not at the forefront of the new science. This led him up more than one blind alley. Though he worked hard to develop his wireless business, the tone of his advertisement in *The Gramophone* of February 1932 tells a sad tale:

'A Question of Policy'
"The Handmade Expert Gramophone was first introduced early in 1930 in order to provide an ACOUSTIC gramophone capable of covering the entire AUDIBLE range of modern recording.

Since its inception no 'Expert' model has been altered in any single detail, nor will any change be made while recording remains in its present form, which, in view of the complications and expense of film recording, and of the vested interests of the big recording companies, is likely to remain for many years to come.

I repeat with emphasis, that my recent activities in the world of radio have only been at the request of numerous customers, who wished to extend the usefulness of their various Expert models and use them as loud speakers for radio work, thus obtaining through the wonderful acoustic properties of the Expert Horn, and the Expert Moving Coil attachment, results far in advance of any ordinary moving coil speaker.

The Expert radio set was introduced simply because my customers - having at hand the high standard of reproduction of an Expert Acoustic Gramophone, - demanded better wireless results than any ordinary radio set could ever give them.."

This text has the ring of an apology about it, and is not the confident statement of a man who believes in his product. For the road Ginn had travelled down was a rather curious one. A moving coil loudspeaker had been developed to fit into the back conduit casting of the Expert Horn. It could either be supplied as part of a pedestal radio-gramophone, or separately in the form of a Senior Horn and casting on its own stand. Expert Radio could then be hooked up to it, and an Expert pick-up could be added to make the outfit a radio-gramophone. The Expert Horn, truer as it was to scientific principles, lacked the

The New 'Expert' Cadet
by
Em Ginn

Its modest price and its neat and compact design will at once explain its purpose to bring the 'Expert' standard of reproduction within the reach of those sincere lovers of good music who hitherto have found it impossible to acquire one of our larger models from considerations of price or size. There is now no need to tolerate the obvious inefficiencies of any type of Internal horn machine, and in the interests of real music we are proud to have removed the last remaining barriers to the enjoyment of all the real quality that recorded music can offer to the music lover of modest means yet very keen appreciation.

£12 10 0

Effective Acoustic System—4 ft. 6 in. Cabinet, Horn, Tone-Arm and Sound-Box hand-made throughout Horn instantly detachable Fits snugly into any corner.

Every 'Expert' Cadet model is made with exactly the same careful testing and tuning as every other 'Expert' model.

Now take your choice
'Expert'
Senior £32 10 0   Junior £22 10 0   Minor £17 10 0   Cadet £12 10 0
Every model Designed and Built by an Idealist Tested and Tuned by a Musician
The one outstanding Quality Gramophone for Home and Overseas.

'EXPERT'
HANDMADE GRAMOPHONES
55 RATHBONE PLACE, OXFORD STREET, W.1

elegance and refinement of the E.M.G. shape, and always looked rather ugly. It could be perhaps tolerated on a gramophone, but as a separate entity on its own stand - it would have competed with the 'biggest aspidistra in the land.'

By the following September, even Ginn had to call it a day, and admit defeat. His advertisement said it all:

<u>'Electric or Acoustic?'</u>

"How many times has this question been debated by potential buyers during the past two years or so, and how many have purchased radio gramophones and have been disappointed? In many cases asking me to take them off their hands in part exchange for an Expert Acoustic Gramophone.

The radio-gramophone is unreliable, and delicate. It relies on hundreds of small connections and intricate wiring, its tonal quality is false, very impressive upon first hearing, but not musical and will not stand critical analysis. Remember, every radio-gramophone purchased today is obsolete before you have had it for six months.."

From this we may infer that in September 1932, Ginn had once more been forced to abandon all attempts to produce a satisfactory competitor to the E.M.G. DR2. Unable to compete in this field, we must assume that he hoped to cover his failure by trying to discredit radio-gramophones in general.

The ever watchful Michael Ginn, now really suffering from the continuing depression, decided that if he could not attack E.M.G. on the electrical side, at least he could hurt them at the bottom of their range. He rushed out a new small acoustic model for the Christmas market of 1932 and called it the Cadet. This was an ill conceived machine, designed to fit the market place, rather than to produce music well. To misquote Congreve:

"Thus grief still treads upon the heels of pleasure. Designed in haste, Ginn may repent at leisure."

Intended to under-cut the E.M.G. Mark IV, by a mere two shillings this little machine reproduced music so badly that it had to be fitted with the larger Minor horn and then it suffered the further indignity of having to have its name changed to Ensign. It brought little pleasure to its owners and no credit at all to Michael Ginn. Its life was understandably and mercifully short.

Another of Ginn's bright ideas at this time was to allow W.J. Bond, the maker of the Cascade 'sideboard' gramophone, to display it at Rathbone Place. Bond was principally a timber and plywood importer, who had come to gramophones via the cabinet making route. He supplied the Expert Committee with cabinets for various pieces of equipment, including the Vox radiogram. Gramophones were little more than a hobby with him to begin with, and the machine which Ginn displayed for him was designed to look like a conventional sideboard, but to sound like a scientific gramophone. It had a straight

internal exponential horn, and its reproduction was pretty good. Bond however was unable to supply his own design of soundbox, so perhaps Ginn tolerated this odd machine to help him sell soundboxes of his own design.

To be fair though, Ginn was not the only one to produce machines of less than perfect design. Balfour Davey was responsible for a large internal horn table model known as the Mark V, or with storage space for 100 records in a pedestal cabinet, the Mark VI. Technical details of this machine have not survived, but from the fact that it was never submitted to the Expert Committee, was rarely advertised by the firm, and appeared spasmodically in the private 'For Sale' columns at the back of *The Gramophone*, we may deduce that it never had the full confidence of its designer, nor the approbation of its buyers.

The endless blasts of propaganda trumpeted from Rathbone Place, coupled to the growth of esteem for the Expert range of acoustic machines, did in the end begin to wear down the long suffering E.M.G. There was still much confusion in the public mind about the difference between E.M.G. and E.M. Ginn: a confusion that Ginn did everything in his power to encourage. Customers were forever asking at Grape Street what the letters E.M.G. stood for. This was hard to deal with, but in time a convenient formula was devised. Staff faced by this awkward question were advised to mumble about 'electrical and mechanical gramophones,' anything to avoid mentioning the accursed name of Ginn! This defensive attitude is evidence of the identity crisis from which E.M.G. suffered at this time.

Reggie Brayne, always on the lookout for ways of overcoming this embarrassing difficulty, could hardly believe his eyes when one day in early 1933, the answer simply walked in through the door. A young designer and artist, a regular customer of E.M.G.'s called Michael Wickham showed Brayne a woodcut he had just done for his own amusement. It depicted a man sitting in an armchair reading a miniature score under the looming horn of a Xa. Brayne asked if it was for sale. Seeing Michael Wickham taken aback slightly, he pressed the question again, and much to his surprise, Wickham agreed, when a five pound note changed hands.

"I was rather naif in those days," Wickham was later to write. "Still am for that matter. A smart agent would have negotiated royalties...." In this way E.M.G. came to own what was to become perhaps the second most famous trade mark in the

Michael Wickham

gramophone world, after Nipper. From February 1933, all E.M.G. gramophones, and Davey radios were to carry an ivorine plate bearing this 'House Mark' as Balfour Davey called it. Owners who had purchased their machines earlier than this date were supplied with an ivorine plate free, on request.

This was an auspicious start to 1933, for the market began to pick up, and E.M.G. was now well poised and able to supply it. With a full range of accessories and machines, and an excellent trade in records and miniature scores, not to mention their other range of electrical apparatus, it was not suprising that they began to prosper.

April found Ginn still struggling. He wrote in his advertisement for that month:

E.M.G. trademark

"Though we take pride in our idealism, we would emphasise that this quality of ours is tinged with sufficient common sense to warrant our continuously experimenting with a view to discovering whether we can yet improve on the most perfect of gramophones - acoustic or electric - i.e. the Expert. So far, nothing we have yet done or seen or heard would warrant our introducing

Some E.M.G. publications of the 1930s.

electrical reproduction, or changing any single feature of the Expert..." This was surely another smoke screen to conceal the fact that they still had not been able to develop anything themselves, with any pretence to quality or reliability. They did still, from time to time offer radios and loudspeakers, but it might have been a rash man who bought one at this time.

Like C.K. Ogden, Ginn suffered acutely from hand to mouth disease. The scope of business was altogether too narrow. As the early months of 1933 went by, Ginn realised that he was going to have to do something radical just to stay in business - and he was going to have to do it quickly.

He found someone else in a similarly precarious state. For nigh on a year, *The Gramophone* had been advertising their top floor.

"Among our readers there must be someone who knows someone who wants just such offices as we have to let at 10A Soho Square. When 'Vox' was started, and *The Gramophone* moved from 58 Frith Street to share new offices in the Square, we thought them the most perfect offices imaginable. Ideally situated from a business point of view, so far as communications are concerned, they have the further advantage of being ideally planned on modern lines, and yet, being in one of the old houses facing south onto the Square with its beautiful trees and view down Frith Street beyond. Ever since 'Vox' came to an untimely end our top floor has been empty... *The Gramophone* meanwhile has been living luxuriously on the other floor.

To be over-housed in these stringent days is a real disability, and we have no excuse for occupying so much space in the heart of London except that of sweet necessity. We shall be prepared to pay commission and present a complete set of N.G.S. records... to any reader of *The Gramophone* who finds us a tenant for our top floor.."

The Gramophone's desperation to find a tenant was only matched by Ginn's desperation to find a friendly landlord, and a cheaper rent. In June 1933 he became *The Gramophone's* first tenant of their top floor. Anyone who has laboured up those four flights of stairs will soon realise just how precarious Ginn's finances must have been, for him to have ever considered taking those premises. They were even more inconvenient than 'The Office' at High Holborn. They turned out to be a big obstacle for customers to overcome, and one could have every sympathy with Edith Sitwell who would arrive on the top floor gasping for breath, throw herself down on the floor and lie heaving on her back, crying, "Oh Mr Ginn, your bloody stairs!" If the years 1930 to 1933 had been difficult ones for Michael Ginn, 1933 to 1936 were to be difficult ones for customers.

The Exhibition of British Industrial Art in June 1933, was a showcase for the best of contemporary British products in relation to their function in the home. It was a real compliment to E.M.G. that Wells Coates, the famous architect/designer wished to design a cabinet specially to house a Davey radio, to make it ideal for installation in a modern flat.

Make a point of seeing

• DAVEY RADIO *at the* B.I.A.
Exhibition of British Industrial Art
Now open at Dorland Hall, Regent St., S.W.1

• *A new and fully descriptive folder now ready showing REDUCED PRICES for Radio-Gramophones.*

Wells Coates, the leading modern architect and pioneer of design in industry, has designed some cabinets specially for Davey Radio, one of which is shown in the photograph. Davey Radio Sets and Radio-gramophones are made to individual requirements. They give a great deal better reproduction and are more reliable than any mass-production article.

E.M.G.
HAND-MADE GRAMOPHONES LTD   11 Grape Street
(*behind Princes Theatre*) LONDON, W.C.2   *Temple Bar* 7166

Perhaps it was due to this event, that Balfour Davey turned his attention to redesigning the cabinets for all Davey radios and radiograms. From 1933 onwards for more that 15 years, their appearance was standardised - quarter cut walnut veneer with ebonised edges.

Apart from these minor changes, the E.M.G. range was unchanged for 1933, with one very important exception. This was the Mark Xb. The largest horn that would pass through a standard doorway was one of 29½ inches diameter, and this was the size supplied with the Xb. At last, E.M.G. had produced a machine which could compete with the Expert Senior on equal terms. As expected, it had no sooner been announced than three months production was fully booked. Those who were waiting impatiently for delivery were titillated by Edwin Evans, musical editor of the *Daily Mail*, who had just been treated to one of the Daveys' tours of Grape Street:

"There is something suggestive of the old craft guilds in the kind of personal craftsmanship exercised at Grape Street. The one (Xb) I heard goes a long way to solving the last remaining problems of the gramophone. In fact the only limitation I could detect turned out to be a defect in the recording, not in the reproduction. The extremes of the gamut, both high treble and low bass came out well, and certain characteristic timbres such as that of the piano, are reproduced with astonishing fidelity."

Two Mark Xbs at home in the music room.

The flush of orders for the new model coupled to a market that was now awakening, enabled Balfour Davey to report that 1933 had been E.M.G.'s best year ever, making more and better gramophones than ever before.

Ginn's move to Soho Square had given him the opportunity of taking a long hard look at his business to see how it could be improved and re-organised to better effect. One advantage of sharing premises with *The Gramophone* was that he was able to rebuild his personal relationships. *The Gramophone* was so relieved to have him as a tenant, and so glad of the rent that past difficulties were soon forgotten. Constant meetings on those stairs enabled Ginn to get a supply of hot information, and to pick peoples' brains too. It was one of those meetings on the stairs that was to cure one of his biggest headaches. He met F.E. Godfrey again. Godfrey too was in the throes of re-organising his own business, and when Ginn asked him to mastermind Expert Radio he accepted with alacrity. Since he had been replaced at Grape Street by Frank Davey, he had been rather out in the cold. Ginn could hardly conceal his delight that he now employed the former E.M.G. radio expert. This arrangement was to have immediate benefits for Ginn. Suddenly, he was able to advertise Expert Radio with complete confidence in his product:

'Expert Radio Sets'

'The great knowledge and experience we have obtained from developing the Expert Gramophone to its present high standard of 'quality' in musical reproduction - a standard to which other forms of reproduction can only vaguely aspire - enables us to offer you a radio set which, 'for sheer musical worth' is as far in advance of ordinary wireless receivers as the Expert acoustic gramophone is ahead of all other gramophones.

In the design and building of these radio sets, we have been singularly fortunate in securing the co-operation of Mr F.E. Godfrey, a name well known to readers of *The Gramophone*, and undoubtedly the greatest authority on 'quality' radio reproduction in this country or any other country today. This happy combination of technician and musician places an Expert Radio set in a class by itself.'

Now that there was no longer any need to deal with the City Accumulator Company, Ginn found another and much better cabinet supplier. In a Dickensian premises over a shop in the Euston Road, Charles Somerbell made cases for scientific instruments. Now he was to make Expert gramophone cases too. These

" *If a man wrote a better book, preach a better sermon, or make a better mousetrap, than his neighbours, tho' he build his house in the woods, the world will make a beaten track to his door.*"—EMERSON.

A special "Expert" Senior, built to the order of a gentleman in Cape Town, South Africa. Horn can be removed in one second. The cabinet of this model is a beautiful example of hand-made workmanship. Personally I prefer something a little more on the modern side, but tastes differ. Incidentally, my cabinet-maker would be pleased to undertake the manufacture of any piece of fine furniture, under my personal supervision.

A special order cabinet still in use in South Africa in 1998.

were a great improvement and now equalled the quality of the E.M.G. ones made by Darrieulat.

It took Ginn six months to complete the re-organisation of the business, and to get it running smoothly. Ginn took on two young men to assemble the acoustic machines, leaving Creese and Phillips to put together the Godfrey radio equipment and tune the soundboxes. The absence of a continuous flow of customers left Ginn with time on his hands, and soon

E. M. Ginn presents the *"Expert"* AUDIO-PLAYER

PURSUING my policy of ignoring compromise and afterthought, I have pleasure in announcing that after many months of continuous research I am now able to present an entirely new type of acoustic musical reproducer. By virtue of the extraordinary quality of its performance it definitely supersedes all existing forms of internal horn type gramophones, but it does not, nor is it intended, to supplant any existing "Expert" model. Its design has primarily been evolved to meet the exacting demand of the connoisseur of music who prefers the appearance of the internal horn type gramophone.

The "Expert" AUDIO-PLAYER will give an added grace and charm to any room, and the individuality of its cabinet work reflects the hand of the master craftsman.

It is my sincere belief that with the return of prosperity the demand for genuine craftsmanship will once again become evident, and I am confident this new model will not only uphold my name but further enhance my reputation as the maker of the finest gramophone in the world.

Within the limits of the adjoining column I have detailed the salient points of the "Expert" AUDIO-PLAYER—and any of my customer-friends are welcome to come and hear this new and unique acoustic instrument.

E M Ginn

Salient Features of the New "EXPERT" AUDIO-PLAYER:

An ENTIRELY NEW instrument for the acoustic reproduction of recorded music—construction differs entirely from all other "Expert" models.

•

Incorporates unique method of sound-wave expansion by the "Expert" TWIN-COUPLED LOGARITHMIC MANIFOLD system which is as startling in its originality as it is successful—a system that at last satisfies the demand for a self-contained instrument of real musical worth.

•

The only internal horn type gramophone in the world that is positively NON-DIRECTIONAL.

•

Although self-contained it retains the wonderful STEREOSCOPIC quality that helped make the "Expert" external horn models world-famous. Until now this effect has never been obtained with the ordinary internal horn type gramophone.

•

Like all "Expert" models, it is HAND-MADE from start to finish of the finest materials available. Every individual part is tested with minute care.

•

A wide range of COLOUR SCHEMES is available and Cabinets may be had in Oak, Mahogany, Walnut, Sycamore, or Maple.

•

Prices range from £16 10s. (excluding stand), and a Special Overseas model in solid Teak bound with brass may be had for £20. Stands range from £2 10s.

E. M. GINN, HAND-MADE GRAMOPHONES, 10a SOHO SQUARE, LONDON, W.1

---

enough the Devil had made work for idle hands. Casting about for novel ways of drumming up business, Ginn came up with what he called the Audio Player. This machine which first appeared in January 1934 was claimed to have 'stereoscopic' properties. (This curious use of the word stereoscopic seems to have originated in 1925 when the German radio station Voxhaus broadcast concerts via twin microphones, each one connected to a transmitter using a different frequency. Where these transmissions were received on head-phones, or on radios tuned to the different frequencies, it was claimed that the result proved that the ear perceives a double effect in the same manner as the eye, when viewing stereoscopic photographs.) In terms of acoustic science it was surely an aberration, which defied all known and trusted acoustic principles. For the man who had built his reputation on machines designed especially for the truth and accuracy of their reproduction: for the man who had championed the external horn, to make a machine with one internal horn would have been eccentric, to say the least. To make a machine with two, seems bizarre. Even Ginn's explanation of the reasoning behind the appearance of this extraordinary machine was lame:

"It has been produced in deference to a number of demands for an acoustic gramophone of small dimensions and pre-possessing appearance with the best quality and range within the limits of the acoustic system employed."

If this obfuscatory explanation means anything at all, it must mean that here was a gramophone specially designed to look nice, to which consideration the acoustic performance had been sacrificed! This statement rings with all the truth of a cracked bell, and we have to look elsewhere for the explanation. In 1928 or 1929, Percy Wilson and George Webb had devised a system of twin horns, which they illustrated in their book *'Modern Gramophones and Electrical Reproducers.'* The twin horn system employed in the Audio Player looks identical. Acoustic science had moved on since then, leaving this experimental design to gather dust. The most likely explanation seems to be that Ginn heard of the existence of the batch of these horns made for Wilson and Webb, and thought that with these he might be

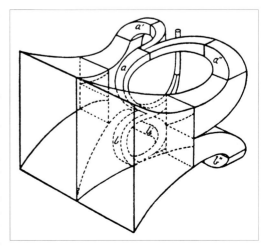

The Wilson/Webb bifurcated horn system.

able to effect sales by their novelty, where he was failing to make sales by science. The Audio Player was not offered for long, probably only as long as it took to use up the small batch of horns!

Fortunately Expert operations were not dependent on the Audio Player for their success. With Godfrey's co-operation, the electrical side began to play an increasing role. On a rising market, Ginn was able to find more customers who were prepared to let him build equipment for them. At last the base of his business was broad enough. Orders steadily increased for acoustic and electrical equipment. By the summer, four years after he had started out at Rathbone Place, he was able to advertise that he had sold 687 acoustic machines. For the first time, Ginn was able to spread jam on his bread, thinly spread, but jam nonetheless.

The rising market found E.M.G. well prepared to take advantage of it, and 1934 was a year of rapid expansion. For the first time, electrical sales overtook the acoustic. Large installations were supplied to the Royal Academy of Dramatic Art, Rugby, Charterhouse, and Harrow, while public address systems were installed in many City churches. Business was now so brisk that Frank Davey recruited Frank Maltby an old Etonian friend of his from the Royal Signals to join the firm. This resulted in one notable improvement to their range of specialist equipment. The E.M.G./Maltby Patent. Electric gramophones could now be fitted with an illuminated graduated scale on the front of the motor board. As the pick-up arm tracked across the record its progress was shown on the graduated scale, thus if the user wished to be able to place the needle on exactly the passage he required, he could now do so, by first playing the record through, then noting where the passage came. This ability to find the passage required with pinpoint accuracy was invaluable to broadcasters, music critics and lecturers on music, as well as students. The patenting of this invention gives some indication of the level of business that E.M.G. was doing with institutional users.

An E.M.G. Mark Xb Export Model gramophone with jointed horn.

The last improvements were now put in place for the E.M.G. acoustic range. Earlier, when shipping costs to the outposts of the Empire threatened to kill off the export of the great horned machines, an 'export horn' had been invented, made in two pieces joined by a collar. This had halved shipping costs, and so safeguarded foreign sales. Ginn, always at the ready to knock anything that came out of Grape Street, immediately condemned this horn, claiming that it produced a deadening effect in the reproduction, at the most critical point in the expansion of the sound waves. Now, Balfour Davey offered the ultimate accessory, the XB, with the oversize horn. The diameter of this horn was nearly 34 inches. It was principally designed for larger than average rooms, which would have to have larger than average doorways. Anyone ordering one of these monsters would be given the treatment by the salesman.

"Thank you for your order sir, now please may I have the address of your field?"

"Er, my field?"

"Yes sir, your field. We deliver the machine to your field, and then you build the house around it."

On the usual basis of 'anything you can do, I can do better,' Ginn now offered his 'All Range' horn of 36 inches diameter or any diameter up to four foot six inches. He did not mention that to achieve this, he had to have the horn made in two parts like the E.M.G. export horn. There was now no mention of the deadening effect... These vast horns were the last exotic flowers of the acoustic age, and were, before many years were to pass, destined to join the Dodo and the dinosaur. The end of the acoustic age was now in sight.

The E.M.G. XB or Oversize horn."Somewhat too large for the ordinary room".

The Expert All Range Horn.

(Like marriage, contemplation of owning one of these over-size machines should not be undertaken lightly or frivolously. More than one new owner proudly arriving at his front door, has been crestfallen to discover that he cannot get the horn into the house by any means at all. Circumcision has been necessary, and when once inside, a second circumcision has been required before the horn can be got into the desired room. Even experienced dealers view these horns with deep suspicion. The excitement of the initial purchase has often been tempered by the impossibility of removing the machine from the room. Windows have had to be removed, complete doors, and doorcases, even in one case a large section of wall. (Was this machine delivered to a field?) However, despite all the difficulties these horns pose, if one can get one installed, by whatever means, the sound of a basso profundo in full song in his lowest register, makes any difficulty seem of no consequence.)

Chapter Seven

Up to the War

The years 1934 up to the outbreak of war in 1939 were destined to be the golden years of the gramophone for both E.M.G. and Expert. The grim years of the depression were behind them. Money and confidence had returned to the market place. With one or two minor exceptions, both firms had now completed the development of their acoustic range, and were concentrating on further development of the electrical equipment. E.M.G. were so confident that their range of products was complete that for the very first time, they issued, in October 1934, a catalogue detailing the full extent of their products and services. This catalogue represents the final realisation of Balfour Davey's vision of what he wanted E.M.G. to become, when he took over management of the firm in

Send for a copy of the new catalogue

From the front cover to the last page you will find it full of interest. Our old customers will be glad to see the evidence of progress we have made in the last few years. New customers will learn with interest of the very wide scope of our business, of which it is literally true to say we cater for *every* requirement for the best reproduction of music from record or broadcast performance. The

Hand-made Gramophones
are fully described with all their measurements, packing charges and shipping costs. We have tried to give the fullest possible information on every point.

A c c e s s o r i e s
are fully dealt with, and there is a page dealing with conversions (the fitting of our components into existing gramophones), an economical way of securing the finest reproduction.

R e c o r d   S e r v i c e
With the Christmas mails soon leaving for the distant lands, it is time to think of friends abroad. And thinking of them, may we be permitted to remind you that our record service will ensure the success of your gift. We stock only the best recordings of all the classical records in the catalogues of H.M.V., Columbia, Parlophone and Decca-Polydor. We issue specially recommended lists and a monthly buying guide. The catalogue gives further information about this service.

E.M.G.
HAND-MADE GRAMOPHONES LTD.
11 GRAPE STREET (*behind the Princes Theatre*)
LONDON, W.C.2

TEMPLE BAR
7 1 6 6 - 7

1930. It had not been an easy road to travel, and the 'Horn Wars' with Michael Ginn had put more rocks in his path than he could have foreseen, but finally he had reached his destination. The emphasis at Grape Street had always been laid on the quality of service, and that quality was now second to none, for the serious music lover. (It is worth pointing out perhaps that only serious music was ever stocked by E.M.G., with the sole exception of Alec Templeton's fugue 'Bach goes to town' played by Benny Goodman. Anyone who dared to ask for a record of jazz or light music unwarily, was discouraged by a supercilious raised eyebrow, or an expression of great pain, but if they were insensitive enough to insist, reluctantly the record could be ordered.)

It might be wondered why the sales of acoustic machines were still so buoyant, when in technical terms they were already obsolete.

E.M.G. XB Oversize.

Anyone who thought their production was only sustained by sentimental 'old buffers' who refused to admit the superiority of the electric equivalent, would be completely wrong. Compton Mackenzie gave us a clue to why this should be as early as April 1933, when he wrote in his *Gramophone* editorial:

"Last month I said that it was a relief to return from electrical gramophones to my acoustical E.M. Ginn Senior Expert and E.M.G. Mark Xa. So it was, but it must be remembered that I make a demand from the gramophone which very few people make. I do not suppose for a moment that the average man, living in average conditions of modern life would prefer an acoustical instrument. It is obvious that a radio-gramophone like an HMV transportable radiogram at 19 guineas is a far better investment for the average man than the more expensive acoustical instrument. Yet, there are still many people living in remote parts of this Earth for whom a radio-gramophone is an impossibility. For those, instruments like the Expert, the E.M.G. and the Cascade are a wonderful substitute for the electric wonders of today..."

It was these very people, 'living in remote parts of the Earth' who were now ordering these machines in such large numbers. Where there is no electricity clockwork must rule. Now that the freight charges had been halved by the provision of the Export Horn, Mark Xs, and lesser E.M.G.s too, and to a lesser extent Expert models began to travel the sea lanes and the dusty tracks of the Empire. The training of colonial officers was usually undertaken at Oxford or Cambridge, where candidates studied colonial law, as well as the language of the country they were going to; here they met, often for the first time, these giant horned machines in the ownership of their dons and tutors. Nothing they had ever heard compared with the astonishing performance of these machines. So, it was hardly surprising that when they graduated and were about to leave the shores of Britain for a lifetime's service abroad, they should want to take with them something that would remind them of home, something that evoked memories of the civilised world they had volunteered to forsake. What could be more nostalgic than an E.M.G. playing Elgar under the black velvet of a night on the African Veldt? It was not just colonial officers who ordered them, of course. Wherever there was a regimental mess, an embassy or diplomatic mission, a wealthy merchant or a religious mission, in short, wherever there were islands of British culture in a foreign land, there these acoustic machines would be found. The whole British Empire resounded to their beautiful voices. They were despatched to almost every country in the world, the fewest going to the United States, where it appeared that the home grown models, with their folded exponential horns were preferred. Nor was it only abroad where there was no electricity. There were still very many parts of the British Isles where this utility had not reached. This fact itself was responsible for a substantial amount of business. Those who moved house from an area which had electricity to one that had not were obliged to have their electric machines converted back to clockwork, and vice-versa. Those moving for the first time to an area with electricity might also wish to upgrade their clockwork models to radio- gramophones. This business kept the workshops busy, and pushed up the price of second-hand machines as well.

Even though Ginn was now doing much better than before, he still cast envious glances at E.M.G.'s record business. He was not yet able to afford to keep a stock of records himself, and after the last occasion when he borrowed money to help him expand, he was naturally unwilling to repeat that mistake. However, this did not prevent him from time to time trying to find ways to make money from record sales, without having to lay out for a stock. At Soho Square, his first venture was evening concerts, with records supplied by Mr Rimington, of Rimington Van Wyck. So many people came to the first one that this venue had to be abandoned and a new one found. The Cafe Marguerite on the corner of Soho Square and Greek Street was chosen for subsequent concerts. These were very jolly occasions, as were any occasions at which Michael Ginn presided, and everyone had a good time, and a cup of tea and biscuits, but as a means of selling records and the means to play them, they were not a great success. The concerts continued for a couple of seasons, and were then quietly abandoned.

Still Ginn did not give up. He managed to get himself appointed sole British concessionaire for a French series of records called 'L'Anthologie Sonore.' This comprised previously unrecorded music from the fourteenth to the eighteenth century. The quality of these records was very high and the series did contain some very interesting pieces, but public interest was low. Compton Mackenzie did try to help Ginn, by giving the series a big plug in *The Gramophone*. He wrote that he would be very disappointed if readers did not order 500 sets. He must have been very disappointed indeed, for after a year, a mere 49 sets had been subscribed, and Ginn was forced to try to sell records individually. When this too declined to a dribble, he handed the concession over completely to Rimington Van Wyck, and this marked his last attempt to sell records.

E.M.G.'s reply to 'L'Anthologie Sonore' was to inaugurate a Treasury of Music series. This occasional series was devoted to rare and interesting pieces of music from all ages, that not only had never been recorded, but had never been published either.

Never one to let a good death pass him by, Ginn was able to derive some good publicity following T.E. Lawrence's untimely fatal accident. Fortunately for Ginn, Lawrence had just bought a complete set of 'L'Anthologie', and more important, had only just paid for it when he was killed. One of the last letters he ever wrote was to Ginn, thanking him for them, and expressing his delight in them. This information was duly passed to *The Gramophone*, which was happy to relate it to its readers.

By the summer of 1935 the Expert business was in better shape than it had ever been. The firm was able to offer a really good quality radio-gram, which received a good write-up in *The*

Gramophone - a machine in which Ginn could have complete confidence. David Phillips was now sufficiently skilled to adopt commercially designed circuitry, assemble it, and by the most careful attention to the performance of even the tiniest component was able to make a machine that was both efficient and reliable. Any difficulties he might encounter would be sorted out by members of *The Gramophone* technical staff who were in and out of the Expert premises daily. Phillips also had become extremely clever at stripping down and rebuilding the 'Meltrope pick-up'. He was able to improve its performance so much, that he established a corner of the pick-up market all to himself for which he became well known, and from which Expert was to garner a good deal of profit. Despite his improved situation, there is some evidence that Ginn still found business a struggle. In his advertisement for January 1936, he writes wearily:

'Speaking with pride as perhaps the oldest advertiser in *The Gramophone*. I thank any readers who by their continued support have enabled me to continue my fight for the Expert acoustic gramophone...'

Increasing business led to an increase in confidence, and this in turn gave Ginn the impetus to find better premises, where the public could find him more easily. The cheap rent had enabled him to keep his little business afloat, but now it was no longer so necessary to put up with those awful stairs. He found a new site not far away at 64, Frith Street. Expert occupied the ground floor and basement only. The ground floor was divided up. There was a front room, which became the shop, behind it was the workshop, with a tiny office for Michael Ginn and the paper-work. The extensive basement contained a small table under a bare light bulb where Esther Ginn was accustomed to sit for hours turning out fibre needles by the thousand.

Beyond that area, there was a long vault which Ginn leased to *The Gramophone*, for storage of all their back numbers. Before the back numbers filled the space, there was also a table tennis table, where members of *The Gramophone*'s staff came at lunch-times to play furious matches against the Ginns.

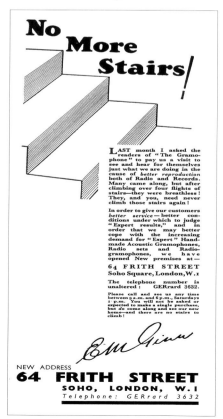

The showroom at Frith Street, was decorated with the trophies of earlier days. There were photographs of Delius listening to his Wilson Horn machine; Ninon Vallin the French soprano, the Sitwells, the E.M.G. stand at the Caxton Hall Congress of 1925, and in a glass case hung the 3 medals that E.M.G. had won in those far off days. On one of the walls there was a large world map surrounded by foreign envelopes addressed to Expert, showing that the firm truly spanned the Earth.

But now came a problem. Joe Ginn was 17 years old and he wanted to join Expert. He had been trained as an engineer at the Regent Street Polytechnic, but the theoretical side had been too much for him. He had been sent 'for hardening off' to a firm in West London. This had entailed getting up at 5.00am and travelling from Highgate, right across London, not getting home again until late in the evening. In time this had made him ill. What he really wanted to do, and in this he had his father's full support, was to go to Horace Hill to work. Hill still did all the metal-work for E.M.G., but when Balfour Davey heard about this, he vetoed it - absolutely. Hill could not afford to lose the business, so there was an impasse. Michael Ginn did not want Joe in the business, probably because he sensed that there might be problems with David Phillips, and probably also because only Michael Ginn knew how slim were the margins. Maybe he did not really believe that Expert had a long term future. In the end, due entirely to Esther Ginn's special pleading, Joe was grudgingly allowed a small basic workshop in the cellar, but on the same basis as Horace Hill at Grape Street. He had to try to earn his living elsewhere, but would have to make what the company wanted, when it was wanted. In exchange for his very modest facilities, he also had to agree to join one of the volunteer sections of the armed forces. Joe chose the Civil Air Guard, where in due course he obtained his pilot's licence.

The new arrangement did have some advantages for Michael Ginn. Joe got himself quite a bit of work from a firm of gun makers round the corner, Wilkes and Co., but they would only pay him in cartridges, which were duly handed over to the boss. Otherwise Joe Ginn's contributions were only occasional. He designed the Expert counter weight, and when customers came in with special requests, he was detailed to oblige them if he could. This often required a certain amount of ingenuity. Bob Bromley came in one day. He was a music-hall showman, who was about to undertake a long tour of Africa with his puppets. He required in a hurry an acoustic machine, but with a volume control. Whilst in the privacy of one's own home, a cushion can be put down the horn, this was not an option for a professional like Bob Bromley. Joe got over the problem by building a butterfly valve into the acoustic system - just an odd job to Joe, but a great service to Mr Bromley. However, as Michael Ginn had feared, Joe's arrival did begin to cause some tensions with David Phillips. Joe, keen to show what he could do on his own, designed a brand new pick-up arm. When he took it and showed it to his uncle, he was dismayed to be told that Joe was not the Expert designer, David Phillips was, and that in future he should stick to doing only what he was told

64 Frith Street.

to do. This was no place for a keen young engineer to be, and it foreshadowed troubles that were to beset Expert later. Though the volume of business was steadily increasing since Expert had moved into Frith Street, one has to wonder whether business would have survived without its dependency on *The Gramophone*. Its relationship seems to have been not so much symbiotic as parasitic. The interconnecting threads were so entangled that it is impossible at times, to separate the two different entities. David Phillips, who represented the electrical enterprise within Expert, still had a knowledge of electrical design that was not completely adequate. He struck up a close acquaintance with Gilbert Wilson, Percy's brother, who was an electrical engineer. Gilbert Wilson supplied the additional expertise that Phillips needed, and was happy to do so. He also encouraged Joe Ginn to be more adventurous in the electrical field. Expert built experimental equipment still for Percy Wilson, including a vast loudspeaker. This was formed from an All range horn extended to four foot six inches in diameter, and mounted on its own baffle. Not only would it not go into the room for which is was intended, but when it was set up in the garden for testing it attracted complaints from up to a quarter of a mile away. The Expert Committee also used F.E. Godfrey to build things for them, and Godfrey also still worked for Ginn. Ginn assembled the electrical components of the Vox radiogram for the Expert Committee, even though these were supplied by Godfrey. The Vox cabinet was built by Ginn's old friend, W.J. Bond. The two firms were almost one.

Ginn, writing of the nature of his business in March 1938 claimed:
'*The Gramophone* and my satisfied customers are my only methods of advertising, and the

fact that I am still in business today despite the competition of big mass production firms, and companies, is ample proof not only of the quality and integrity of Expert products, but also of the intelligence and discrimination of the readers of *The Gramophone*.

I of course build standard models of acoustic gramophones, radio sets and radio-gramophones, but, because every Expert product is handmade from start to finish I am able to give personal attention to the EXACT requirements of each individual customer, and therefore my various models are standard in name only.'

The real nature of the Expert business seems to have been rather different. Ginn would listen very carefully to the needs of his potential customer, and good salesman that he was, he would soon convince him that he could build it exactly as it had been described. Then, with the design brief clear in his mind, he would consult David Phillips, who would consult Gilbert Wilson, until the design could be built and tested. Sometimes other designers were consulted, a man called Donatti for example, but a great deal of help   from outside was actually needed to enable Expert to continue in the bespoke radio and radiogram business. From time to time they still got requests to make truly eccentric items, such as the radiogram that had to be made to resemble a miniature 19th century pipe organ. (Was this another commission from Lord Berners?).

Ginn was used to dealing with the great and the odd, but even he must have been hard pressed not to blink or giggle, when, one day, a Mr Leach came into his shop. Leach was a retired cotton mill owner, who had recently lost his wife. He lived in Colwyn Bay. He had been making determined attempts to contact her by means of a spiritualist church. A short time before he turned up in Frith Street he had attended a seance where the medium claimed that she was in communication with a Red Indian called Red Cloud. She kept up a stream

Expert Pipe Organ radiogram.

of apparently irrelevant messages, all meaningless to Leach, and then, all of a sudden he heard the words he had been longing to hear. "Is there a Mr Leach here?" She repeated this a couple of times. Leach made himself known, and waited breathlessly. Instead of the intimate communication he had expected, Red Cloud merely said: "If you are thinking of buying a gramophone, you could not do better than call on Mr Ginn in Frith Street, London."

Leach turned to Ginn, and said "I wasn't but now I think I will." And so he did..

In due course David Phillips and Joe Ginn were despatched to Colwyn Bay to install the machine. It was a long journey (it must have seemed a very long journey in the Ginn's 1927 Morris van) and when they got there they were very tired. They installed the machine, and set it up, making sure it was level, ensuring the soundbox was tuned exactly correctly for the room, and that everything else was just as it should be. After supper they went to their room. Just as they were about to turn in, Leach knocked on their door. He wanted to tell them that if they should hear loud knocking in the night, not to worry, as it would only be his wife trying to 'get through'. It was a long sleepless night.

The strangest thing about this story is that it was true. There may be an explanation however. Gilbert Wilson was a convinced spiritualist, while Percy was sceptical. As an amusing intellectual exercise, Percy eventually designed some scientific tests that he believed could completely disprove the spirit existence. The only trouble was that when he undertook the tests, they appeared to prove exactly the opposite. Percy became a believer too. They abandoned seances shortly afterwards because every time they summoned a spirit something unpleasant happened to either one or the other of them.

It just seems too much of a coincidence that Gilbert Wilson was a personal friend of David Phillips, and Ginn too for that matter, and that Leach should have been so accurately directed to Frith Street. But then, we live in a cynical age!

Meanwhile, E.M.G. continued to do good business at Grape Street so good in fact that they were able to reduce the prices of several of their machines. Even so, they did not become complacent, and were still keen to improve their services. In 1936, they were able to offer certain Telefunken records, now pressed in Britain, and they introduced Davey Record Dressing. Their announcement of the introduction of this product is particularly interesting, for it shows their continuing determination to offer only those products which had a sound basis of good science:

'A new and important discovery':

'Since the earliest days of the gramophone, waxy and greasy dressings of various kinds have been applied to gramophone records. Such dressings have been placed on the market in the past but these were mostly messy to apply, tedious to play out once applied, and liable to harbour dust and dirt. With the introduction of graphite, these older methods have largely disappeared.

Being equipped with a laboratory, it occurred to us that we might usefully look into the chemistry of waxes to discover what were their essential virtues in their application and how disadvantages and even dangers might be avoided since it was clear that the matter had never been systematically investigated.

It became apparent at once that there were enormous differences in the properties of waxes, ranging from the very valuable, to the highly undesirable from our point of view, and it was not long before we had good grounds for hoping that with a correct choice and apportionment of materials a record dressing of singular value might be produced.

The results of our experiments have exceeded even our own expectations..'

E.M.G. also offered Record Cheques, as they called them, and new forms of record storage, from permanent but flexible shelving units, to the 'Ready Rack' holding twenty records, enough for a day's listening. The firm also managed to get hold of a set of four privately recorded HMV records of Madame Susan Metcalf-Casals, to which they had the exclusive right.

A peak of business was reached at Grape Street in 1937, from which E.M.G. was gradually to descend. In this year, alarm bells began to sound more urgently across Europe. The name of Adolf Hitler became a household word. At last, the National Re-armament programme was initiated which led to an immediate shortage of some strategic materials. This shortage soon spread to virtually every sphere of production except military production, and the gramophone business suffered with everyone else. There was one highlight though for E.M.G. Frank Davey won the contract to equip T.O.M. Sopwith's new motor yacht, Philante, with a Davey Radio-gramophone installation in every

cabin. Reggie Brayne, after seven years with E.M.G., now left, not only leaving E.M.G., but the gramophone business which had employed him for fourteen years. The grim business of preparing for war soon resulted in rising prices, which coupled with shortages led to a constriction on production.

Ginn too had been enjoying his best years since 1930. Customers came to Frith Street who would never have dreamt of climbing all those stairs at Soho Square. A passer by outside his shop in the years before the war would have easily recognised many of his customers, who represented all branches of society and the arts. Augustus John, Eileen Wood, and Mantovani would have rubbed shoulders in the shop with less famous people, among these a customer of whom Ginn was particularly proud. This was the postman from Hampstead, who had saved and saved to buy the object of his desire - an Expert Minor; which he wanted more than anything else in the world. With better access to technical advice, Ginn was

Michael Wickham's E.M.G. Mark Xb.

able to offer three standardised designs of radios and radiograms, and towards the end of 1937, he offered Radiant Diffusion radio, which he defined as a radio set which was able to produce soundwaves simultaneously and unobstructed from all four sides of the cabinet at once. Radiant Diffusion was achieved by placing the loud-speaker on its back facing upwards into a cone, which directed the soundwaves equally in all directions. To be really effective the radio on its stool had to be positioned in the centre of the room. This people were not prepared to do - and the idea though original, lapsed.

Already though, there were signs of slackening demand. Fishing for business with more than his usual bravado, he offered to build almost anything imaginable; battery sets, sets for DC mains, amplifiers, speakers, baffles, public address systems, cabinets, pick-ups and even 'an outfit up to £200 to include television.' All of this he claimed could be built at short notice. If it could be built at short notice, it must have been because he had a short order book.

Uncertainties pervaded 1938 with business reduced, but still possible. E.M.G. introduced a cheaper range of radiograms the DR7 and DR8, and added the last pre-war accessory to their extensive list - Davey Thorns for pick-ups and lightweight soundboxes. Some people began to doubt that war would really come. Ginn, unwisely as it turned out, was in optimistic mood in January 1939:

"I personally am confident that the days of crisis National and Financial are past and that this year will see a return to Integrity and Stability in our daily lives."

*Stuart Lockhart with a DR7 in one of the audition rooms
at Grape Street.*

By summer, the evidence was all too clear where the government's opinion lay. Soho Square was equipped with air-raid shelters, and a sandbagged ARP post, to which *The Gramophone* donated a box of records, and the Gramophone Exchange a portable to play them on - on raid free nights.

Michael Ginn and his family decided to shut down Frith Street for good. All the contents that they thought worth moving were transported to Ingerthorpe again, which was to become the home of the Expert for the duration of the war. The last room to be cleared was Michael Ginn's office. Joe Ginn can remember his father going through all the files, letters and testimonials of which he had been so proud. Savagely he tore them up, one by one. Joe pleaded for the letters from T.E. Lawrence, in the names of Shaw, Ross and Lawrence, but his father refused, ripping them apart without mercy, saying that they were just rubbish now. When all written history of Expert handmade gramophones had been destroyed only the medals and photographs being spared, Joe and his father took a last look round the building, and then locking the door for the last time, walked away.

Chapter Eight

The War Years

Following the declaration of war in September 1939, E.M.G. issued a terse communiqué:

"Many of our customers have written to express the hope that we shall be continuing our business as usual during the war. We are taking this opportunity to thank them for their good wishes and to assure them that we are still to be found at Grape Street. We have for the time being lost the services of Mr H.B. Davey who has returned to the RAF and of Mr F.G.G. Davey who has returned to the Royal Signals, and of other members of our staff."

In those early days of the war, those who had military training and experience either volunteered or were called up from the strategic reserve, and posted according to their competencies. Balfour Davey, much to his disgust was thought to be too old at 45 for operational duties, and so was obliged to spend the early months of the war seeking sites for airfields, and surveying them. Later, he was doomed to administrational duties for the duration of the war. Frank Davey, as a boffin, was first posted to the Royal Signals Research Establishment at Malvern, where he was appointed Deputy Commandant. When the V2 rockets became an unwelcome feature of the southern skies, he was sent to Harrogate to set up a series of signal interceptor stations to monitor German communications from the Pas de Calais. This intelligence gathering was a vital part of the greater operation aimed at cracking the secrets of the German Enigma code machine, perhaps the single most important intelligence operation of the whole war.

M18 masterminded this operation from Bletchely Park, in Buckinghamshire. Here the British genius for original thought was pitted against the super logical efficiency of the German mind, and as history has subsequently shown, conquered it. The deliberately odd mixture of people from widely different backgrounds and disciplines was a cocktail of originality that proved too strong for the enemy. Amongst this motley collection of genius, which included a professor of astro-physics, several statisticians, some economists, writers, language masters, lawyers and others, was a stockbroker - namely Horace West, whose war up to then had been a series of episodes of farce.

In 1938, when Chamberlain had returned waving his famous piece of paper, Horace West had rightly concluded that war was both inevitable and imminent. He tried to join a London territorial anti aircraft unit, but they were, even then, fully subscribed. He had to settle for the nearest alternative, and was sworn in as 2061434 Sapper West, in 306 Company London Electrical Engineers (Searchlights.) As he later observed: 'A Victorian upbringing followed by 5 years at an army school (Wellington) with two corps parades a week provided a good grounding as a private soldier in time of war.'

For months this training unit was obliged to do all its drill without any equipment at all. Finding imaginary aircraft in the night sky with imaginary sound locating apparatus and imaginary searchlights proved an interesting if surreal experience and the outbreak of war perhaps came as a welcome return to the real world, for with the war came, as if by magic, their equipment.

After a spell of duty at various sites in Eastern England, Sapper West was surprised to be summoned peremptorily to the War Office. Here he was offered the chance to join a new intelligence unit that was then being assembled, and this offered the chance of a commission. However, though he leapt at this opportunity, at his searching interview it emerged that he was not the right West. Now, there was a real problem. Here was an ordinary sapper, who had by accident been allowed to penetrate the outer defences of perhaps the most secret outfit in Britain. He was obliged to remain to work with M18. Instead of dismissal, he was commissioned.

In due course, he found himself at Bletchley Park, where he became immersed in information gathering techniques. In 1943, without warning, he was posted to India: 'Send West by fastest means available,' the message had read. His posting led to an outbreak of hostilities between the army and the Foreign Office, as anyone who worked at Bletchley

Park was forbidden to travel abroad, for obvious security reasons. This problem was eventually overcome. There followed a tortuous journey by Sunderland seaplane from Ireland to India, by way of Portugal, Gambia, Nigeria, Belgian Congo, across Africa to Egypt, Palestine, and down the Gulf to India. This journey took thirteen days. West arrived at New Delhi only to be met with blank stares. The post he had been summoned to fill with all haste, had long since been filled, and he was not required. This debacle resulted in a much more congenial posting to Eastern Wireless Sub Centre at Barrackpore near Calcutta, and from there a prolonged tour of the operational sites along the Burmese border. (Among many places he visited, was Imphal, where Compton Mackenzie could recall seeing a vast E.M.G. horn lying abandoned in the British Residency building after the siege of Imphal by the Japanese.) By now he had risen to the rank of acting major.

As the Japanese retreated southwards, the E.W.S.C. lost its purpose, and Major West joined another unit, where he took responsibility for dropping agents into French Indo China (Vietnam) behind enemy lines, and collating any reports that were subsequently received. Here, much to his surprise, he came across another E.M.G. colleague, Col. Frank Maltby, who was similarly engaged.

With E.M.G.'s staff officers distributed across the world, back at Grape Street it was left to the other ranks to keep the show on the road as best they could. The calm of pre-war days soon returned, the shop became a centre of civilisation in a world gone mad. The sandbags in the street were the only visible evidence that Grape Street was at war. Tom Fenton, who had joined the firm in 1929, now ran the shop, and was given the unenviable task of recruiting replacements for the staff who had gone to war. It was he who was responsible in 1939 for recruiting the first woman ever to work for E.M.G. She was Quita Chavez, who brought to the firm a specialist knowledge of opera. Feeling in 1942 that she wanted to do something of more immediate value to the war effort, she joined the army. At her interview she was asked where she worked. "At E.M.G.", she replied. "Well, you must have a very good ear," came the response, and she was posted to Queen Ethelberga's school in Harrogate, where soon enough she discovered her commanding officer was none other than Colonel Frank Davey.

The business manager was Geoffrey Parsons, who now had overall responsibility for the whole E.M.G. operation. There were few changes to begin with, the war seemed hardly to affect the firm, save for the loss of staff from time to time. The firm still stocked a complete range of records, and miniature scores, and quite a number of books. The supply of machines became patchy due to shortage of materials and perhaps more to the point, a shortage of technicians to put them together. Curiously, even the Telefunken records, which E.M.G. was allowed to press from the German matrices, were still available.

It was inevitable that sooner or later, the effects of war would be felt but it was not until the autumn of 1940, a year after the war had begun, that E.M.G. began to feel the squeeze. The 'Limitations of Supplies (Miscellaneous) Order' restricted the sales of everything except records to a six monthly quota. Packing materials, essential for a record business, began to be in short supply. Purchase Tax was introduced at 25% and the firm ran out of record albums. The *Monthly Letter*, previously supplied free, now, had by law to be charged for. In January 1941 they suffered the first really serious inconvenience. The *Monthly Letter* and *The Art of Record Buying* were delayed by the destruction of their printer's premises by enemy action. It is hard to imagine just how difficult it was to keep going at all. The Blitz was at its height.

This was the year that saw the total destruction of the Queen's Hall, and the devastation of many of London's most familiar landmarks. The loss of the Queen's Hall was felt with particular sadness at Grape Street.

Twice it had suffered bomb damage. On the 8th December, 1940, bomb blast blew out most of the windows and doors, and again on the 6th April 1941, but the 'coup de grace' was delivered on the 10th/11th May 1941.

'For five moonlit hours over 300 bombers dropped great numbers of incendiaries and high explosives, causing a serious fire situation, setting a new record for casualty figures

(1,436 killed, 1,792 injured) and doing great damage to public buildings. The House of Commons Chamber was destroyed, Westminster Abbey was hit, as were the British Museum, The Law Courts, The War Office, The Mint, The Mansion House, The Tower..' The list seemed endless.

The staff of E.M.G. had to clamber daily over the remains of buildings blown into the street, piles of fallen masonry, burnt vehicles, sometimes corpses, but they still came to work every day. Tom Fenton was called up for National Service in October 1941. He served as a fire watcher for the rest of the war as he was not fit enough for active service. He still continued to write the *Monthly Letter*, though from time to time, he allowed a little irony to creep in.

'We apologise for the late appearance of this issue,' he wrote in October 1941, 'which is chiefly due to the difficulty of listening to records with critical attention while the nightly barrage is in progress.'

A footnote recorded that E.M.G. had now released 18 of its male employees for National Service.

The shop was closed for a week over the Christmas period, to allow the hard pressed staff to get out of London and enjoy a few nights of peaceful sleep. It was quite usual for the staff in the weeks before Christmas to work from 9.00 am, until the small hours of the following day; no small sacrifice, when the dark nights offered the Germans the best chances to drop their bombs. The firm still felt it of the utmost importance to process every order, and to answer every letter before closing for the holiday.

The peculiarly intimate E.M.G. service was not restricted either to those who bought things from the firm. There was genuine concern for those whom the war had deprived of their enjoyment of serious music. From early in 1942, E.M.G. by means of the *Monthly Letter* tried to establish contact between those who were still at home, and in possession of their gramophones, and those in the forces who had been separated from theirs. Customers were encouraged to write in offering musical comforts to the deprived. It was a most kindly thought, and by this means many in the forces were offered real solace. Recently, in the summer of 1996, a gramophone concert was being given in the Manor, Hemingford Grey in Cambridgeshire, on a Mark Xb. At the back of the music room, sat an elderly American. When the concert was over, he approached his host, and thanked her. He was deeply affected by the concert, and amazed too. He said he had first come to that house in 1944,

The Expert Senior at The Manor, Hemingford Grey in 1942....

when he was an airman stationed nearby. The only thing that he could see that had changed in all those years, was that in 1944, the concert had been given on an Expert Senior, while today it was on a Mark Xb!

The screw tightened further. The 'Limitations of Supplies Order' now included records, restricting their manufacture, and limiting their sale only to regular customers; in the case of E.M.G. this meant only the takers of the *Monthly Letter*. Packing materials became ever scarcer, also the quality of the records received from the factory was rapidly worsening, as the experienced pressers had all gone to war. The staff was now so small, that the shop had to be closed on Mondays so that those who remained could deal with the build up of correspondence. In May 1942, Parsons had to close the shop for a week as even if one person went on leave, the business could no longer function. John Amis has given a marvellous description of what working in the shop was like at this time in '*Amiscellany*'

(Faber 1985) and it is interesting that when he asked what E.M.G. stood for, he too was mumbled at about Electric and Mechanical Gramophones. Even twelve long years after the 'Great Schism', the name of Ginn was to be avoided at all cost. Truly, the wounds of the 'Horn Wars' ran deep and suppurative.

Purchase Tax was doubled in May 1942 and packing materials were no longer obtainable at any price. The *Monthly Letter* explained: 'Some of our customers have been distressed to find that having called to collect their records, they must carry them away unwrapped, the penalties for supplying bags or wrapping are very severe, and string is very scarce...' There was some good news though. E.M.G. were able to offer a small stock of HMV portable machines 'to those in the forces and others who are parted from their E.M.G.s.'

Eventually, Geoffrey Parsons too was called up. The few remaining technicians in the workshops drifted away to war, until there were none left. (One was

... and with Mrs Lucy Boston.

killed in an air-raid - the only E.M.G. casualty of the whole war.) This led to the unlikely circumstance of David Phillips returning to Grape Street to help them out. He was there in 1942, when a new lathe was delivered (probably to enable E.M.G. to undertake some minor government contract, to help them keep going.) George Overstall, better known to gramophonists as the other half of Bratley and Overstall, soundbox makers, saw Phillips there, when he was sent by Melhuish, the makers of the lathe, to supervise installation. Phillips almost certainly helped with the tuning of soundboxes and radio repairs. As during the war a batch of E.M.G. soundboxes was made in unplated brass, while brass was a proscribed material, it is more than likely that the lathe did not work exclusively for the government, and that unwittingly, the government supplied the precious brass.

Tighter and tighter turned the screw. In the autumn of 1942, following the Japanese capture of Singapore and Burma, supplies of shellac reached an all time low. The British Legion mounted a national salvage campaign in an attempt to recover from old shellac records material for new. A standard price was offered all over the British Isles - four pence for a 12 inch, and 2^1/2 pence for a 10 inch. It was intended that when these old records were bought, the grooves should be scored through before returning them to the factory. Quita Chavez observed that many record collections of E.M.G. staff greatly increased at this time. Customers were encouraged to bring in some wooden record boxes, so that the postal record trade could continue, 'despite their suitable size and shape for the storing of seed potatoes' as the *Monthly Letter* said.

The supply of Davey needle cutters ran out and could not be replaced, so the last two remaining cutters were firmly chained to the wall. Purchase tax increased to 100% on new records, though E.M.G. were still able to supply a choice at pre-war prices. The shop had to close for ten days over the Christmas period of 1942, as the firm had sold all its quota of goods.

Matters continued to deteriorate in 1943. Now, even to get your quota of new records, you had to send back 75% of your order in used records. Several more of the staff were called up. There was still no packing of any sort. The shop again had to close for a week at the end of August, due to shortage of staff. 1944 was no better either. Staff were now so short, that customers were warned that it might become impossible for the firm to answer any correspondence. A further four million salvaged records would be needed, and supplies from this source too were declining to a dribble. The shop had to close for two weeks at the end of August 1944. There was by now nothing left to sell. The firm managed to limp into 1945, now little more than a shoestring business. The end of hostilities in Europe was noted laconically in the Newsletter:

'This has been a year of great achievements in the world of recorded music, as well as in other spheres.'

If the years of the war had reduced E.M.G. from a highly prosperous business, to an anaemic and emaciated ghost of its former self, Expert had fared no better. Michael Ginn had volunteered to return to the army, while David Phillips took up a post of incident warden in Highgate. He had been trained pre-war, and was one of the few fully trained professional wardens. This was a taxing job which left very little time for running a business, even if he had been capable of it. In 1942, he received a peremptory summons to attend a nearby RAF station, where he was required to sit exams in circuitry, as the RAF was now desperate for radio technicians. He passed this exam with ease, and waited with some disquiet for a letter to arrive calling him up. Instead he was called to the Town Hall, where he was given the news that he was indeed required by the RAF. It was pointed out to him that he was too valuable for the civil authorities to lose either, so what was to be done? Phillips, with his usual cunning left the choice to them, gauging they would put self-interest above the national, and he was right. So he stayed where he was, but he tried to do some repairs to oblige old and loyal customers. From time to time he was able to assemble a machine from the small stock of pre-war parts, and parts robbed from machines taken in part exchange, but in the main Expert went into hibernation until the end of the war.

Michael Ginn's war was unexciting too. He was 40 in 1939, and as he had had no fighting experience at all from the last war, he was thought too old to be of much use. The army managed to keep him occupied for a couple of years, as a security officer at Newport Docks, but he was then de-mobbed. Straightway, he volunteered for the Navy. This entailed some delay in the processing of his application. Determined to be useful to the war effort in any way he could, he found a job with Horace Hill's widow, May. She was under government contract to supply all sorts of machined parts, and Ginn took the job of negotiator, middleman between May Hill engineering and the government buyers. Finally, the Navy found Ginn a place, and he spent most of the rest of the war teaching officers to shoot rifles.

The last member of the Expert team was Joe Ginn. With his experience gained in the Civil Air Guard before the war, it was natural he should join the RAF. Though he gained his pilot's A licence, he was not in the end chosen as a pilot for operational duties. He spent the war as a corporal fitter-armourer, and loathed every minute of it.

Michael Ginn, RN

Chapter Nine

Expert - The Post War Years

Michael Ginn was demobbed on the 10th November, 1945. Though he had enjoyed his war, he was looking forward to returning to civilian life. More than anything he was keen to breathe new life in to Expert, after six years of commercial inactivity.

It was soon only too obvious that things were somehow different from before the war. There was an 'atmosphere' at Ingerthorpe that had not been there before, and it made him feel uneasy. Nobody would say what the trouble was, and he could not exactly put his finger on it. When he attempted to discuss the shape of the new business, David Phillips was evasive. When Ginn persisted, Phillips became irritable. They got nowhere. It was not a happy beginning.

It was Esther Ginn who made the first move. Once again she got down to making the bamboo needles - by the thousand. It was not much, but it was a start. While the men growled testily at each other, packets of needles began to pile up. The sale of needles, unobtainable during the war, enabled the firm to rebuild contacts with pre-war clients. This in its turn led to a small volume of repairs and tuning business which at least kept David Phillips occupied. It was not until March 1946 that Expert was able to offer any new equipment - a brand new amplifier design at £30, but it was only an offer. There was absolutely no hope of delivery, as there was no wood for cabinets. In June they were able to express the hope that an amplifier ordered now, might be able to be delivered by December. The situation was hopeless. Although needle cutters, and thorn sharpeners did become available once more, feelings of frustration and gloom descended on Ingerthorpe.

The reasons for the unwelcome atmosphere gradually began to become clear. During the years of the war, David Phillips had had life organised more or less as he wanted. Life at Ingerthorpe had been relatively easy, as he was in effect kept by his mother. He felt more confident now too, for he had had a responsible job for the first time in his life, and he had held it down. He had also had a great deal of time in which to think. He could see quite plainly that the future belonged to electrical reproduction, and that he was the only one who had the relevant knowledge, either to design and make, or to repair equipment. The only question he could not at that time answer was whether or not he still needed the Ginns, or would he end up by having to carry them?

Matters were not improved by the arrival home from the war of Joe Ginn, in 1946. He too was looking forward to returning to work, preferably with Expert. The sight that greeted him on his return was not quite what he had expected to find. He too at once encountered the sour atmosphere, and was disappointed. Then, the once elegant drawing room was filled from floor to ceiling with broken radios. These belonged to customers of an air raid warden colleague of his uncle's, who had dumped them at Ingerthorpe hoping that somehow they would get repaired. Joe was anxious to clear some space for his workshop, so he began to try to repair them. This unleashed his uncle's wrath, so he was obliged to abandon the project. Joe's appearance did have one immediate effect. His uncle now insisted that Expert should be reconstituted as a Limited Company. This was partly due to the uncertainty of the times, and partly to define his role in the company. He was now no longer an employee, he was the technical director. Michael Ginn was still managing director and Esther and Joe ordinary directors.

The continuing shortage of materials led to a general deterioration in personal relationships. There was far too much time in which to nurse grievances, and far too little to do. They all got under each others' feet. Phillips grew increasingly jealous and resentful.

Another year was to pass before there was any real improvement in the supply of materials. Phillips continued to design new equipment, until the Expert range was quite impressive, but it was only theoretically available. It took until the summer of 1948 before anything approaching a full menu of goods could be both offered and supplied. A two piece record reproducer was now offered in various forms from £100 - £154, and the very last acoustic Expert Senior described as a 1947 model. Even then it must have looked like a dinosaur.

In anticipation of work that was never really to materialise, Joe Ginn set up a range of small workshops for himself. There was one in the attic, one in the coal-hole, and a plating plant was established in a wash-house out at the back. The dining room was now cleared out and workbenches put up. These were fitted with line shafts to drive various machines. From time to time he was asked to supply the chassis for Expert amplifiers, but often he was put to work repairing Rothermel Crystal pick-ups, under the jaundiced eye of his uncle. This was grindingly boring work, but it did bring in a few pounds every week.

Expert came very close to being closed down altogether about this time. A letter was received from the agents of the Church Commissioners saying that they proposed to make a thorough inspection of the premises. This caused a panic. The house was only held on a domestic lease, and if any evidence was to be detected that it was being used for extensive commercial operations, they might all be in serious trouble, even possible eviction. It was impossible to remove all traces so a plan was made. Joe was to camouflage what could not be removed.

"The camouflage I put up," he recalled, "was almost an art form. I removed all the line shafts and pulleys in the down stairs workshops, and hung Expert Senior horns all over the bearing brackets. The machinery was covered with old sacks and baskets, wood etc., to look like junk". When the agent arrived, he was given a guided tour by Michael Ginn and was doubtless subjected to his most sparkling wit and charm. The result was that the visit passed off without adverse comment and Expert was, for the moment, safe. It had been a near thing.

In December 1949, a formidable rival of Expert, H.J. Leak and Co., published the results of a test undertaken by the National Physical Laboratory of their triple loop 12 watt power amplifier. The principal feature of these results was the very low level of harmonic distortion that they had achieved - 0.1% at 1000 cps, and 10 watts output and 0.19% at 60 cps, and 10 watts output. Michael Ginn sensed that here was an opportunity for a publicity coup. He consulted the grumpy David Phillips about whether he could outdo this remarkable achievement.

With his well known predilection for the quest for perfection, coupled to a low work load, he decided to have a go. He undertook this task with his customary thoroughness - not from an extensive base of theoretical knowledge, but a painstaking attention to detail. As Percy Wilson had remarked years before, the secret of a good gramophone lay in the balancing of its components, and so with this amplifier. Starting from a commercially available circuit, Phillips obtained the best quality components he could lay his hands on, in some quantity, and then set about construction. His skill lay in the realisation that although it was the manufacturers' intention to mass produce the components, in reality, their individual performance varied significantly. By testing each tiny component in the circuit, for its performance in relation to the others he was able, bit by bit to eliminate imperfections. This process was naturally impossible for any ordinary commercial undertaking to contemplate, but it was right up David Phillips' street. The final version was in due course submitted to the NPL and they awaited the test report.

When it came, the results surprised and delighted them all. The levels of harmonic distortion had been reduced to 0.02% and 0.05% at 1000 cps, and 60 cps, respectively. Michael Ginn had been right to choose this ground for his public demonstration - it had been a brilliant success. The euphoria at Ingerthorpe could not however disguise the fact (not mentioned publicly) that the Expert amplifier based on the NPL tested design, was much more expensive that H.J. Leak's. Whether any customer could have noticed the difference in performance must be seriously doubted.

Early in the 1950s David Phillips' mother died, and left the lease on Ingerthorpe to him. Now, his grumbling complaints found a new and more forceful voice. He began to make open threats that he could, and indeed might, fold up the company. The premises were his, the useful knowledge of design and manufacture were his, and the shortages of the market place would sell anything he might make. He did not need the Ginns. This was a bitter pill for Michael Ginn to swallow. Meal times became acrimonious board meetings, at which all the frustrations tended to be aired, but without the unction of tact or diplomacy. The fury which was unleashed, and the disillusionment which flowed from it, drove Joe Ginn away, much to the chagrin of his father. Joe set up a workshop of his own under a railway arch at Muswell Hill where for a time he made some small parts for Expert, but he was sustained by Horace Hill's widow, who gave him a steady flow of work. After a while, he ceased to make anything for Expert, though he retained his nominal directorship.

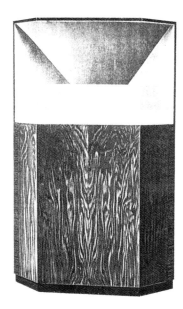

A selection of Expert products of the 1950s.

The personal crises at Ingerthorpe were temporarily shelved when the long playing record appeared. Expert found that suddenly there was a huge increase of work. Very many customers required their equipment to be converted; new three speed motors, amplifiers to be retuned, speakers to be redesigned, and much tuning of complete conversions. It was a shot in the arm for the ailing business. The new flush of business awoke the old Ginn flare, and he turned his mind to sales again, with new found confidence. He invented 'Binaural Listening'.

Whether this idea was a further development of his ideas of non-directional sound diffusion, begun with his audio player of 1934, or whether it was a splendid wheeze for selling twice as many loudspeakers; or a combination of both, must be left to the reader's judgement. The new found confidence can be felt in the flow of classical Ginn prose, setting out the argument for this new idea:

Binaural Listening:

"This is a thrill that, once having experienced, you will never forget. It consists of using two perfectly matched Expert loudspeakers of exactly similar characteristics, one in each opposite corner of the room. The perfection of binaural listening is of course achieved by the use of two Expert Master speakers. This needs a large room and a lot of money, but the quality of the performance is indeed truly remarkable. One listener called it 'uncanny.'

The room is simply flooded with sound and it is quite impossible to pin-point the actual source of the sound. This does not mean you have to play at full volume, quite the reverse. Of course you can use as much volume as you wish, you will not offend the ear, but a high volume is not necessary or desirable. The great success of two Master speakers used in this way, led us to experiment with our other speakers, and we found that two specially matched Expert 'All Range' speakers were equally successful, but there again, our room is a large one, and the 'All Range' speakers cost £40 each.

We were determined that the wonder of binaural listening should be able to be enjoyed by those who have a small room and who do not wish to pay more than £25 for the extra speaker. This led us to experiment with two of the latest Expert 'Acoustic Column' speakers, both specially matched and the result far exceeded our greatest expectations. We started by standing a speaker in opposite corners, as before and the effect was truly magnificent. We realised however, that not every housewife can permit two corners of one small room to be used to house loudspeakers even though they are quite unobtrusive, so we tried standing the speakers one on each side of the fireplace, and they not only looked very good, but sounded wonderful. We then tried standing the speakers in various positions in the room with equal success. The great secret of binaural listening is the exact matching of the two speakers. It is not enough to take two exactly similar speakers by the same maker and consider them as 'matched'. Every speaker unit made has slightly different characteristics, and it is only when subjected to careful tests on proper scientific instruments that one realises how very different two exactly similar units by the same maker can be. These differences have to be overcome by us, and not until we have 'doctored' each unit and adjusted them until they are a perfect match, both on our instruments and to the ear, do we consider them good enough for binaural listening. Should the response of the two units or the cabinets in which they are fitted vary in the slightest degree, binaural listening will not be a success, quite the reverse. This 'matching' and testing takes time, and time is costly, but once you have experienced binaural listening as offered by Expert, you will agree that it is well worth while."

The brightness of the creative light that emanated from Michael Ginn, was now that of a guttering candle, flaring before it flickers and dies. The world outside Ingerthorpe was changing faster than they could react. Mass production which for so many years, they had scorned as a provider of high quality, now had reached the stage when the difference between good quality and very good quality was slight. The numbers of people who required the superb quality of Expert, and would be satisfied with nothing less, fell away. All the responsibility for financial matters lay on Michael Ginn's shoulders, and he felt the weight of it. The firm had no capital. When it could produce an outstanding piece of equipment it could not produce it in quantity, and so reap the rewards of its design. Employees of sufficient ability could not be afforded so others had to be used who were less qualified. All around them, other firms were mushrooming, able to produce high quality equipment at factory prices. Expert could not compete in this world. As the 1950s advanced, the market continued to be more and more hostile to makers of bespoke equipment, especially those who were undercapitalised. The absence of City premises became an ever greater hurdle to jump. Money worries mounted, and desperate measures had to be contemplated. Recitals of recorded music were offered at Ingerthorpe, as they had been at Rathbone Place and Soho Square, but this time, the response was flat. In another attempt to re-establish an Expert presence in the heart of things, demonstrations were arranged in conjunction with Webb's Radio in Soho Street, but there was little interest. Expert equipment still continued to attract superb reviews in *The Gramophone*, and sales were still made around the world, but the volume of production could not be raised so as to rescue them from the mire into which they were sinking. They tried to work in co-operation with firms like Burne Jones, and this too failed to improve things. By 1955, matters had become so desperate that the firm advertised that for the first time, they were establishing a dealership, rather curiously situated in Belfast, Adelaide and Eastbourne. It was all too little, too late. Michael Ginn had tried everything he knew to save the firm, but all to no avail. The strain finally broke him. In 1955 the first ominous signs appeared, and in 1957 he suffered a massive stroke. He lost his power of movement, and he lost the ability to speak. Bereft of his customary vitality, he was taken to the geriatric ward of the Whittington Hospital, where he was to vegetate for two long years.

David Phillips, who for so long had threatened to exclude the Ginns from the company as unnecessary, now, faced with the chance of running the show on his own, backed away from the responsibility. It was Esther Ginn who, in July 1957, had to make the decision to sell the firm. The name was bought by Wolsey Television Ltd. a subsidiary company of the Gas Purification Group, who also owned Grundig. Esther Ginn was appointed company secretary, and her brother, technical director, both under S. Duer, the general manager.

Although the Expert name remained in existence, the ethos of the firm evaporated all too soon. Duer's management style was flashy. The products were no longer handmade, the service no longer so personal and exclusive. The quality which had been the hallmark of Expert was no longer there. The take-over was never the success all parties had hoped for. At first the company traded from Grundig House in New Oxford Street, but as the quality declined, so did the prestige of the addresses from which they traded, until Expert's final address was in an upstairs office in a back street at Thornton Heath.

A.C. Pollard of The Gramophone with David Phillips at the opening of Heathkits in Gloucester circa. 1959.

There the name of Expert Handmade Gramophones finally died.

On February 17th 1959, Michael Ginn died, released at last from his most distressing condition. *The Gramophone* noticed his passing:

"His many friends both among our readers and in the industry will be sorry to know of the death of Mr E.M. Ginn on the 17th February. As founder of the E.M.G. and later of the Expert gramophones his name had become familiar to our readers from our earliest issues.

At the Gramophone Congress in 1926 (sic) his Magnaphone won a high place and the reputation of his firm was enhanced A few years later, he began to market his now famous external horn gramophones. When electrical reproduction came on the scene, he was among the first with his brother-in-law Dave Phillips to change over. In recent years, Expert pick-ups, amplifiers and loudspeakers have won a deservedly high reputation. For the last two years, he had been in hospital, paralysed and bereft of speech. His passing is therefore rather a mercy and a relief than a matter of sorrow. Nonetheless, we offer our condolences to Mrs Ginn and her son and daughter."

His will disclosed that there was nothing to leave behind. It made the point that the contents of the home, within Ingerthorpe, all belonged to Esther, and that his own personal estate was under a thousand pounds. Like Balfour Davey though, he left behind something much more valuable than mere chattels. He left behind his reputation.

It seems rather ironic that his favourite aphorism, much used in his advertisements, was Emerson's: "If a man write a better book, preach a better sermon, or make a better mouse-trap, than his neighbours, tho' he build his house in the woods, the world will make a beaten track to his door." He had trusted this principle, and it had mostly worked well for him. His Magnaphone, when he had perfected it and made it available in 1924, was indeed a better gramophone. His concept of the handmade scientific gramophone led him to make machines which reproduced music as it had never been heard before. As long as he did that, the world did indeed make a beaten path to his door. When he moved out of London back to Ingerthorpe, the path to his door became a long one, and the much despised mass producers had learnt to make equipment of an almost equal quality. Thus the path became gradually abandoned and overgrown. As David Phillips put it:
"In the end, the world closed upon us."

Michael Ginn was always a man who believed that the means justified the ends. Just as he was prepared to use and misuse facts to make a strong argument, so he was not over fastidious about bending the rules to achieve his objective. With the gramophone, his objective was purity of reproduction. For a man who was both unmusical, and scientifically ill equipped, necessarily, he was obliged to rely on others to help him towards his goal. It was his unique ability to charm the knowledge and skills out of them, that gave him the edge in the market place. By means of David Phillips' famous ear, and later, anyone else who could be induced to help, he was gradually enabled to approach the realisation of his dream. This single minded quest for excellence often blinded him to the need for reward and recognition that was due to those who assisted him so generously, forming the rungs of the ladder that carried him upwards. Many who helped him neither needed nor wanted any reward, financial or otherwise, content to help him in the interests of improving the gramophone, but there were those whom he should have rewarded. It was his failure to distinguish between the two that was to cost him so dear.

In the cynical world of today, it would be all too easy to dismiss Michael Ginn's contribution to the gramophone industry as little more than the ruthless exploitation of the knowledge of others, for his own benefit - nothing but sheer opportunism. This would be as unkind as it would be untrue. For many years he did make the best acoustic machines then available, and arguably the best soundboxes. After the war, despite all the enormous difficulties and disappointments the post war years brought him, Expert equipment still maintained a reputation for quality that was the envy of many competitors. Though in the end Expert disappeared, it was as much because Michael Ginn was no longer there to guide it as any other single cause. The nearest a man may get to immortality is the reputation he leaves behind him. When music lovers remember Michael Ginn, and raise a glass to his memory, they should couple his name always with outstanding quality, and be grateful for it.

What then happened to David Phillips? The quest for perfect sound reproduction to which he had devoted the whole of his life, proved a fickle mistress, and a poor provider. After the final demise of the Expert name, he moved to Teignmouth. No financial rewards accrued to him, and there was no company pension, so he was compelled to work to the end. In the winter he still made top quality loudspeakers to private order, and in the summer? Holiday makers, queuing on the front at the little hot dog and teas stall, never guessed that the sallow old man serving them once had the most famous ear in the gramophone business.

Chapter Ten

EMG - The Post War Years

At Grape Street, the beginning of the peace brought little immediate benefit. What materials for manufacture of equipment were available were prohibitively expensive, and it was difficult to know whether to snap them up at any price because they were there, or to wait in the hope that the prices would soon come down. Staff drifted back from the forces and had to be paid, while stocks of everything ran down still further. Because of the state of the economy, export orders to the USA had to receive priority, which caused even more shortages and frustrations to E.M.G., and their customers. It was April 1946 before orders for soundboxes could be accepted. It was July before the DR4, DR5, and DR7 were back in production. Orders were solicited for the Mark Xb and the Mark IX, but the Mark IV was to be discontinued 'once existing stocks have run out.' It was hoped that orders placed in July could be honoured by the following December. Cabinets were the problem. New workshops were taken in Rochester Mews, Kentish Town, where all the assembly and repair work was to take place.

The gloom about delivery dates turned out to be more pessimistic than was really the case, but they were gloomy and dreary times. Some timber did become available for cabinets, and this enabled E.M.G. to step up production of the Mark IX to meet an unexpected rise in demand. The Mark Xbs that were made at this time are usually found with a painted finish to cabinet and horn. This concealed a hotch-potch of different woods, different veneers, and a lack of finishing papers for the horns. Even though purchase tax had been reduced to 25% again, the new price of these two acoustic models had risen by 1946 to £65 and £45 respectively. Balfour Davey's year end report reflected the dour climate:

"For our company, 1946 has been a year of re-organisation and struggle against heavy odds... 1947 will be better."

1947 was better, but only marginally. The year began with a most depressing reduction in rations, meagre enough at their present levels: less bacon, less meat, and no end in sight for bread rationing. Coal too was further restricted, just as a spell of cold weather settled over the whole country, unprecedented since 1891. Then the snow fell, and froze, and fell again until it was impossible to distribute any coal at all. The nation shivered miserably. The *Monthly Letter* tried to put on a brave face:

"Owing to the fuel crisis no new records for March from the EMI group... perhaps in the circumstances this is as well, since the appalling weather conditions, the fuel cuts, (with voltage drop that seriously affects electrical reproduction of records) the mental shocks which daily followed each other have rendered February a month during which the enjoyment of music has been almost impossible."

This year also marked the beginning of the end of Tom Fenton's association with E.M.G. He had been with them since the latter days at Holborn, and even though he had built a high reputation for himself and the firm, and his knowledge of music and recording was unparalleled in London, many of the post war changes were not to his liking. For some time, Balfour Davey had been seeking new ways of adding even more authority to the firm's reviews of new records, and in 1947, he approached Mr Hubert Foss. Foss was a music critic of the highest order. He had worked for the *New Witness*, *The Daily Graphic*, he was correspondent for the *Daily Telegraph*, and *Manchester Guardian*, and he was the head of the Music Department of the *Oxford University Press*. It was a tribute to the status of E.M.G. that he felt able to accept the invitation to become their reviewer, but it was a source of great resentment to Tom Fenton. After all, had he not attracted customers like Adrian Boult who came specially to consult him about recording techniques? There were other causes for his grumpiness. The appointments of Stuart Lockhart, as personal assistant to Balfour Davey and John Job as senior assistant in the record department, left him dissatisfied and disgruntled. Both of them were from the Royal Signals, and both seemed to enjoy Balfour Davey's confidence more than he did.

The last accessory that E.M.G. had added to its range of products before the war had been Davey thorns, for electric pick-ups and light soundboxes. Now, Frank Davey invented and patented the Davey Rollright thorn sharpener This neat and beautifully engineered little gadget used the power of the turntable to drive a carborundum wheel, which in turn sharpened and profiled the thorn. (The name Rollright was a play on words. The Daveys' aunt, Baron Davey's sister, had married the Reverend Henry Rendall, who was vicar of the parish of Great Rollright in Oxfordshire. Among their nine sons was M.J. Rendall who was to become headmaster of Winchester College just one year before Frank Davey went there, and doubtless the reason he was sent). It seemed almost as if the war had been a mere hiccup in the process of constant improvement of services by E.M.G.

A selection of E.M.G. accessories.

If there was a continuing attempt to improve their services to customers, it was not matched by any real upturn in business, and this was a matter of ongoing concern for the directors. The record trade was beginning to improve, as the industry gradually got back into gear, but the other facets of the business were in the doldrums. Though two completely new amplifiers had been designed and stocked, the firm was now obliged to offer equipment made by others. They even stocked HMV televisions. All too often though, there was not enough work to keep the workshops busy, and technicians were often to be seen, standing by their benches, waiting for work to come in. As 1948 opened, EMG thanked its customers 'for their patience and kindliness under many disappointments...' and added, 'shortages and difficulties must continue to beset us...' Behind the scenes though the board was being forced to think the unthinkable. Grape Street was becoming increasingly expensive both to run and to rent, and it no longer really fitted the business as closely as it should. With the manufacturing side now moved out to Rochester Mews, the top two floors were almost unoccupied. After a period of agonising, it was decided to abandon Grape Street, and seek a more suitable and cheaper building.

On April 10th 1948, the doors of Grape Street were closed for the last time, and the task of moving the contents to the new site began. They had settled on 6, Newman Street, and the Daveys were determined that even if it was a smaller building than the firm had previously occupied it should have as magnificent an interior as the firm could afford, and purpose built to their requirements. There was some dispute amongst the directors about just exactly what the firm could afford. Horace West tried his best to discourage what he saw as profligate expenditure. He managed to get the Daveys to agree to his asking the City accountants Mann, Judd and Gordon to cast their eyes over the plans and the firm's recent balance sheets, to see if the expenditure could be realistically met. Looking at a photograph of the interior of the new shop nearly fifty years later, he was to observe ruefully 'I don't seem to have restrained them very much do I?'

The interior of Newman Street with Ted Perry, Alfred Marks and Joyce Reah (overseas orders).

The Daveys won that battle, for the new building was sumptuously fitted. Some idea of what the interior was like can be gained from the advertisement of the opening.

'Here in our new showrooms, beautifully designed and equipped, you may inspect our unique range of electric and acoustic gramophones to much better advantage... most modern audition rooms comfortable, soundproofed and air conditioned... there are six audition rooms on the ground floor, demonstration rooms on the first floor, where electric and acoustic equipment of our own and other leading makers can be seen... Here you may obtain the most objective advice.. on the improvement or reconstruction of instruments of all makes. All standard electrical instruments available for prompt delivery'.

The directors had clearly taken a brutally realistic view of where the future of the firm lay. They had recognised that it would never again be possible to sell only equipment of their own make and design - it was simply too expensive in the penurious post war world. Even though this was the right, and possibly the only decision possible, it did mean that the exclusiveness of E.M.G. had begun to be watered down. The firm had become more like other firms which supplied equipment. Now it was only the record side of the business which was still conducted along exclusively traditional E.M.G. lines.

Customers made no difficulties about coming to Newman Street, and business soon began to pick up. This gave the firm the confidence to abandon finally the manufacture of acoustic machines, whose great horns would forever be associated with them. Out with the old, and in with the new, seemed to be their policy now. All the remaining acoustic parts, and the few horns and cabinets that remained at Rochester Mews were now shelved to gather dust. This break with the past, proved the final straw for Tom Fenton. With twenty years service to E.M.G., which made him by far the longest serving member of the team, he had perhaps hoped for some promotion, even a seat on the board, in the new scheme of things. When he realised that his long service was not to be rewarded he left to work for a friend of Balfour Davey's, Teddy Norris at The Gramophone Shop, in Sloane Street. His departure might not have caused much consternation at Newman Street, had not Teddy Norris announced that at The Gramophone Shop, Tom Fenton would be writing *Fenton's Letter* which would be a critical appraisal of all new record issues circulated to all their customers. This was a blatant attempt to emulate and compete with the *Monthly Letter*, and this act of betrayal must have caused Balfour Davey considerable hurt. He need not have worried though, for E.M.G.'s stature vastly exceeded Fenton's and from that point Fenton's

career declined. He was not happy in Sloane Street and so took a repairer's job with Expert at Ingerthorpe. After a time he left them, and was last heard of as a general repairer of radios and gramophones in a shed at Thornton Heath.

(The question has often been asked "How many acoustic machines did E.M.G. make?" This is a question that up to now could not be answered, as no records of the Company survive at all. However, just as this book was about to go to the printers, a letter from Balfour Davey turned up. It was written to a customer who had asked exactly this question, in 1962. Davey replies that he cannot find any records of how many of each model were made, but he adds that from memory they made 150 Mark Xs, 75 Xas, 50 Xbs, some with oversize horns. If one bears in mind that many, and perhaps most Mark Xs and Xas were later converted to Xbs by the addition of 29½ inch horns and Xb soundboxes, these figures

are probably reasonably accurate. This gives a total of Mark Xs (of all sorts) of 275. As we know that more Mark IXs were sold than Mark Xs, say 350, and that as many Mark IVs were sold as Mark IXs, another 350 this makes nearly a thousand machines. The Wilson horn model, Mark VIII must have been produced in considerable numbers if David Phillips

E.M.G.

LONDON'S SPECIAL GRAMOPHONE SHOP

★ **STANDARD**
and
LONG-PLAYING

RECORDS
for the **CONNOISSEUR**

The record department of E.M.G. Handmade Gramophones, to-day under the personal supervision of Mr. John A. Job, continues to maintain the lead it has held for nearly thirty years in meeting the requirements of those who prefer serious music. Every effort is made to ensure that the finest recordings are available, and the sales-staff are themselves most knowledgeable both in matters of music and of recordings and they can be relied upon to help whenever necessary. Electrically equipped audition rooms enable records to be heard properly, a fact which helps enormously in choosing. There are also available accessories and books about music invaluable for the complete enjoyment of recorded music. In fact, the whole business of trying and buying records from E.M.G. is a pleasure not to be missed by those who love music.

★ *Specially equipped audition rooms for playing the new L. P. discs.*

The Music-Lover's Monthly Guide to Record-Buying
For over twenty years "The Monthly Letter" has regularly continued to provide record-collectors with impartial and authoritative comment on the new issues of records. To-day this publication, which is an independent E.M.G. production, is the most depended-upon of its kind. It is an invaluable guide to those who wish to be informed not only in detail about the latest issues, but how such issues compare with previous recordings, where they exist.
A twelve-months' subscription costs 7s. post free.

E.M.G. HANDMADE GRAMOPHONES LTD.

6 NEWMAN ST., OXFORD ST., W.1

Telephone - - MUSeum 9971 - 2 - 3

correctly remembers making 17 in one week. At 50 per month, say for 6 months this might give a figure of 300. We may only guess how many Mark VIIs were made but surely not more than 100? Add about 100 Magnaphones and 25 others of assorted types - and we arrive at a total production of around 1500 machines).

Ted Perry also joined E.M.G. in 1949, he had called in on the off chance of finding a job. By convincing everyone that he knew the record catalogues backwards, he got one, as assistant behind the record counter. He soon rose to the post of record buyer for E.M.G. (He is now Managing Director of Hyperion Records.) Anyone who worked for E.M.G. at this time, found the E.M.G. connection a passport to higher things, and this is some indication of just how highly E.M.G. was regarded for its in-depth knowledge of the classical music scene. A glance at the career of some of the others who worked there about this time bears this out. Veronica Slater and Helen Young who both worked behind the record counter for a time, went on to become senior BBC producer, and executive in the NZBC respectively. Derek Lewis who was to replace Ted Perry in 1956 became head of the BBC record library. Tristram Cary who worked with Balfour Davey for a time, is now a composer in South Africa. Even those who did not pursue careers elsewhere, were pillars of the musical community in London, like Joyce Reah, who dealt with foreign orders and despatch, and doubled in her own time as secretary of the Philharmonia Choir. Veronica Slater, who came to E.M.G. from Imhofs, was asked at her interview by Balfour Davey, the opus numbers and keys in which the Beethoven quartets were written, and got the job because she could answer correctly. After that she hardly ever saw him again, despite working at Newman Street for two years or so.

A glimpse of the working atmosphere at Newman Street comes from Joan Shirley (now Mrs Holmes) who worked there from 1949-1953:

"The shop staff consisted mainly of John Job, Ted Perry, Veronica Slater and myself. We

The Newman Street record counter with Ted Perry (centre) and the first long-playing records, from U.S.A. exhibited as a curiosity.

were all very happy working there and there always seemed to be a lot of laughter. We did very little of what I call work when the shop was open; we seemed to spend most of our time chatting to the customers, many of whom became real friends, and selling records which we never regarded as work. That started after the shop was shut at 5.30. Then we got down to ordering records and miniature scores, answering letters, checking off new records and putting them into our own record sleeves. We rarely finished before seven o'clock, sometimes specially as Christmas was approaching, it would be nearer nine.

Occasionally, Mr Davey would come from his office - he never seemed to go home at all - and take us to dinner at Berterelli's, an Italian restaurant about five minutes away.

Mr Davey was very tall and spare, he had a moustache and he wore glasses. He was slightly pop-eyed and very quietly spoken. He was somewhat absent minded and had a faint air of expectancy about him. He was forever sending us little chitties as he called them, and we reckoned he couldn't break the habit from his RAF days. Mr Davey always seemed on the verge of floating away. His brother Colonel Davey was quite different, there was a family resemblance but he was much more solid and earth bound.

Tristram Cary, son of the author Joyce Cary, worked with Mr Davey for a while; he was also a composer and wrote some of the music for 'Dr Who', though that was of course much later. Ted Perry called him 'Fetchan' as his surname was pronounced 'carry'- not to his face of course, and the name stuck. I wonder if he ever knew?

There was one chap who wrote record reviews for one of the national papers, who used to come in on a Saturday morning about 12.30 - we closed at one - and take all the month's new records and a copy of the *Monthly Letter* down to one of the audition rooms and write his record review.

Also, there was a customer who used to come in, take one or two records down to play, then bring them back later and leave. He always had a briefcase with him. It was sometime before we realised that he was swapping new recordings for old ones. But suddenly we started finding records on the shelf which we didn't stock, mainly because they were not good recordings and had been superseded by more recent versions. We did eventually nobble him but were rather disappointed when Mr Davey refused to take the matter

From left to right: Joan Shaw, unknown, John Job, Ernie the Packer and Ted Perry.

any further. He said it would be bad for business. However, I believe he 'phoned the other West End shops and warned them to keep an eye out for him.

I remember one occasion hearing a very fast and somewhat high pitched recording of one of the Beethoven symphonies. It was obviously an LP being played at 45 rpm. We waited for an irate customer to come out and complain. Instead, a young fellow came out absolutely in raptures over this marvellous recording. The best he had ever heard, he said. We hadn't the heart to tell him he'd been playing it at the wrong speed."

The arrival of the Long Playing Record in 1950 brought a tremendous amount of business. There was a sudden demand for new equipment, and a great quantity of conversion work on older outfits. E.M.G. had to re-design much of their range to play the new type of record, the DP4 pick-up was modified to play LPs, becoming the DP4/33, and Frank Davey produced his infinitely variable Steep Cutting Filter.

The 1950s saw an ever increasing range of new E.M.G. machines and equipment, new speakers, corner reflex speakers, amplifiers, radios, even a portable radiogram with spring motor, which could also run off a car battery. The firm was still building equipment to a standard of excellence, and not to a price, a pre-war attitude unsustainable for long in the increasingly competitive market. Previously the workshops had lost money because there was insufficient work to keep everyone busy. Now, at last, they were in full production again, but they still lost money. It was a puzzle that worried the directors a great deal over a long period, but try as they might, they could not identify the causes. In an attempt to overcome this difficulty, Frank Davey decided to diversify. He began to work on a micro-wave intruder alarm. Though years ahead of its time as a concept, it was dependent on valves which made it bulky, and it never seemed quite to reach that standard of reliability that would have ensured for it a commercial success. It tantalised him for years. He was determined to overcome its deficiencies and so devoted more and more time to it. He managed to get some of his most advanced equipment into Buckingham Palace, and into a nuclear arms store in Wiltshire, but it failed to obtain the Establishment's unqualified approval. While he pursued the chimera of perfect reliability, his brother grew resentful at the apparent waste of time and energy, and considerable friction built up between them.

Like all firms which build to a standard of excellence and not to a price E.M.G. supplied its customers with equipment that was of an unequalled quality, at what was really a bargain price, although the initial cost seemed astronomical at the time. It is worth mentioning that E.M.G. equipment of the late fifties and early sixties was some of the very best ever produced, and it represents one of the few unexplored areas for treasure hunters. Not only is the reproduction of this equipment amazingly pure, and arguably still the best way to enjoy mono and early stereo recordings, but by the addition of some inexpensive gadgetry, it is possible to play CDs through it. This produces a sound of such breathtaking quality, that it is beyond the power of words to describe. All of this can be enjoyed at minimal expense, if one is fortunate enough to track down some second hand E.M.G. machinery.

Another pre-war attitude which continued to prevail at Newman Street, was the generous latitude allowed on customers' credit accounts. Balfour Davey clearly thought it ungentlemanly to write to customers to draw their attention to their growing indebtedness to E.M.G. Thus, there were many customers who took advantage, whose accounts grew to unacceptable levels. These bad payers were to contribute increasingly to E.M.G.s difficulties.

It was not only the constant worries about the losses from the workshops that had kept Balfour Davey at his desk late into the night. It was his style of management. His first question when he arrived each morning was "Who is in today?" E.M.G. customers were in effect his family, and it was a matter of real personal interest to him who was in the shop. His aim was still the same as it had been when he first formed the vision of what E.M.G. should be - it was to give the ultimate personal service. He left no stone unturned in the provision of this service. He thus imposed upon himself the task of reading and signing every letter that left the building addressed to a customer, specially as he wrote most of them too. It was an enormous task, and it is not surprising that it kept him at his desk late into the night. Some idea of the minutiae with which he concerned himself can be gleaned from a file of correspondence I have between E.M.G. and a customer in Dorset. It covers many years, and details the gradual conversion of what began as a piece of Expert electrical equipment, to an E.M.G. design. There are letters here about such things as the size of a split-pin, a scratch on the cabinet and how to get rid of it, and the non-availability of a tiny spring. Every letter is written and signed by Balfour Davey, except those written whilst he was in hospital, when Stuart Lockhart stands in for him. It was truly a service that no other firm thought it worthwhile to provide, yet it was the very bedrock on which E.M.G. had been built.

In March 1964, the proposed ending of Resale Price Maintenance prompted E.M.G. to publish what turned out to be a prophetic advertisement. It showed the Newman Street premises as a record supermarket, offering heavy discounts on record prices. This clearly reflects the alarm which this proposal caused them. If RPM was to go, records would become the subject of a price war, which they simply could not afford. If their record business was to come under threat, while the workshops were still losing money, they would have no business left. This alarming idea forced them to look ahead and try to plan for the new world on whose threshold they now found themselves.

It was a bleak prospect indeed. If this threat became reality, they would almost certainly have to retreat from Newman Street, abandon their workshops, and look for very much smaller premises. Whilst they pondered these grave questions, perhaps because of the gravity of their situation, Balfour Davey suffered a stroke in October 1964. He was in hospital for many weeks. He went for his convalescence to a nursing home in Seaford, where Mrs Job helped him back to recovery. On their long walks by the sea, he reminisced about his days in the Royal Flying Corps, and the early days of E.M.G., but sadly, the detailed content of these conversations has been long forgotten.

Frank Davey had effectively ceased to be an active director by this time, so management of the firm fell to Job and Lockhart, as long as Balfour Davey stayed away. However, it was not until 30th October 1967 that they moved to 26, Soho Square.

This building was a mere shadow of E.M.G. past glories. Though it had some elegant architectural features on the first floor, the utilitarian and rather pinched look of the shop-front, gave the building an air of mere commercial function. It was, as insurance companies used to say, a saleshop, a place of commerce. Though the firm retained a small capacity to repair machines for customers, the abandonment of the workshops, and the whole of the manufacturing and design function and sales of equipment made the whole concern more profitable. The scope of the business was now much reduced so that in effect it only sold records, record albums, and record tokens. At the heart of the business was still the *Monthly Letter*, with its pithy and authoritative reviews, on which E.M.G. customers had come to depend completely. Gone were the air conditioned audition rooms, and the displays of electrical equipment. The only remnant of the past was a solitary Mark X standing in the window, and even this had to be bought from a customer, as the remaining stock of acoustic machines and horns had been taken away and burnt when the workshops at Rochester Mews had been closed down.

Soon after the move to Soho Square, Balfour Davey was working late into the night poring over the accounts. His desk was lit by a single lamp, the rest of the building lay in quiet darkness. Without any warning, this frail and courageous old man was seized from behind by intruders. They roughly demanded to know where the money was. It was useless to explain that there was no money, that it had been banked at close of business, and that it was mostly cheques. He was tied up, hands behind his back, hands to feet, and thrown on the floor. He was savagely kicked and beaten until he became unconscious. As it had always been his habit to stay on late at night, as he was a bachelor, and as it was Friday night when this happened, there was no one to give the alarm. He was not discovered until the following Monday morning, when a cleaner found him. He was rushed to the Middlesex Hospital, where he was treated for broken ribs, multiple contusions, and almost certainly hypothermia and shock. He was 74 years old at the time.

With the death of Frank Davey in 1968, and his brother only able to attend Soho Square sporadically, management of the business in effect passed completely to John Job and Stuart Lockhart, who were now directors, though technical ownership remained with Balfour

Davey, because he not only had his original shares, but also those left to him by his brother. H.H. West still had the £100 of shares he had bought in May 1930, which had never paid a dividend in all those years.

The business that Job and Lockhart managed was now a good one. There was a large and loyal clientele at home and abroad, but inevitably the years began to take their toll. As this customer base gradually declined, and competition from rivals increased inexorably, squeezed by the jaws of circumstance, the turnover began to decline. In 1972, on May 12th, Balfour Davey died, aged 78. *The Gramophone* gave him a generous if inaccurate obituary.

"E.M.G. is a set of initials that spans more than one generation of readers. It was in 1928 that E.M. Ginn and H.B. Davey set up in business as E.M.G. Handmade Gramophones. Both were perfectionists, and both were destined to go their separate ways. Now the death of Mr Davey will leave a gap in our gramophone friendships. Davey had three great passions in life; aeronautics, music and the gramophone. He served in the RFC in the First World War, and in the RAF in the second. His acute ear, which was to serve the industry so well, could identify most aircraft by sound. For Davey, the gramophone was an instrument to reproduce music, rather than to make it, and because High Fidelity has gone beyond its proper station, and in itself is a meaningless and vulgar phrase he would probably have disliked the label. The quality of sound in its relation to music was the ideal to which he devoted his life. There must be many of his customers who became his friends and whose ears were opened by this dedicated man, whose acoustic gramophones with their external horns lasted right through the 78 rpm period. He has left a thriving business, which in the hands of J.A. Job and R.S. Lockhart will continue to maintain the standard he set".

Balfour Davey passed from this world as quietly as he had lived in it. His will decreed that:

"My remains are to be cremated, my ashes scattered. It is my wish that there be no ceremony religious or otherwise, and particularly no music. My executors should attend my funeral, but the time and place thereof shall not be notified to my relatives until after it has taken place."

As in life, so in death, he was self effacing.

Despite his wishes, there was one lone family mourner at his funeral to see him pass. He left behind nothing that survives except his RAF wartime suitcase with his service number on it, and the altimeter from a German plane he shot down nearly sixty years earlier; nothing that is except E.M.G. and its reputation. His personal contribution to the recorded music industry was so quietly made that there is only a handful of people round the world who have even heard of him. Yet as the acoustic and electrical branches of sound reproduction advanced side by side, it was his range of acoustic machines that set the standard that for many years the electrical pioneers sought to emulate.

John Job and Stuart Lockhart inherited Balfour Davey's shares, and had every intention of continuing as before, but the national economy was hostile to the small business. The collapse of property prices in 1974, the tight monetary controls brought in by the Labour government both removed money and confidence from the market place for several years to come. Here the firm's accounts tell the story better than words.

1974	Turnover	£144,785	**1975**	Turnover	£160,008	**1976**	Turnover	£153,383
	Exports	£ 17,876		Exports	£ 22,916		Exports	£ 24,288
	Gross profits	£ 15,638		Gross profits	£ 13,368		Gross profits	£ 5,507

1977	Turnover	£139,464	**1978**	Turnover	£130,156
	Exports	£ 21,743		Exports	£ 17,473
	Gross profits	£ 96		LOSS	£ 213

Two little anecdotes from these last days of E.M.G. give a flavour of the atmosphere that pervaded the building at Soho Square at this time. H.H. West came into the shop and made the mistake of asking for a piece of music by Prokofiev which he called 'The Love for Four Oranges'. He was regarded coldly by an assistant who raised a superior eyebrow and replied in a very flat voice: "I'm afraid we have only three oranges in stock."

Andrew Keener, who worked for E.M.G. during the last six months of its existence can remember overhearing a brief exchange between Stuart Lockhart and Robert Layton.

26 Soho Square.

Lockhart remarked sadly that E.M.G. simply could not afford to give its subscribers (to the *Monthly Letter*) a 10% discount to which Layton replied with equal sadness: "Can you afford not to, Stuart?"

This question was the awful dilemma which faced E.M.G. in those last days.

When the firm began to lose money, Frank Davey's widow Jean bought some shares as a way of putting what little money she could into the firm, to try to keep it afloat. It turned out to have been a vain hope. Faced with a 300% rise in rent, rising costs, and evaporating profits, John Job, as the senior partner saw closure as the only option. This decision may have been coloured by the fact that he himself had suffered a small stroke some years earlier. Closure was not an option that was acceptable to Stuart Lockhart. He was appalled that Jean Davey should have suffered the loss of her investment. To Lockhart, as it had been to the Daveys, E.M.G. was his life, his family, his everything. Bitter arguments and raised voices made no difference to the inevitable outcome.

The title page of the 1980 *'Art of Record Buying'* reads:
"1980 is the golden jubilee year of E.M.G. Handmade Gramophones Ltd, with the *Monthly Letter* reaching its 50th year of publication. This makes the 1980 edition of the *Art* very special."

It was more special than anyone realised when it went to press. Shortly after it appeared, the doors at Soho Square closed for the last time, and E.M.G. went into voluntary liquidation. When all the sums had been done, and the final balance sheet prepared, E.M.G. paid its creditors exactly 2.6p in the £1.

Although its body corporate had died, E.M.G.'s reputation for service and machines of exquisite quality will surely last for a very long time. To those fortunate few who are privileged to listen to music by means of an E.M.G. machine, the names Frank and Balfour Davey will remain for ever among the immortals, and the letters E.M.G. will remind us of a standard of service whose like we shall never see again.

Tailpiece

.....and finally... what on earth is this?

Appendix I - Soundboxes

David Phillips was solely responsible for the development of the E.M.G. and Expert soundboxes. Starting as a child with his taped up cigarbox, with a needle hammered through the base, he moved on by steady stages to the ultimate perfection of the acoustic soundbox, the Expert dynamic of 1935. From 1929 onwards we have a number of different models from which we can clearly deduce the way his mind was running. The early years of experiment though remain to some extent shrouded in mystery.

The reasons why this should be so are really quite simple. In the first place, very few early E.M.G. soundboxes are known to have survived, and of those that have, there seem to be nearly as many types, as there are boxes. The position is further complicated by the fact that the firm recommended customers to return their boxes twice a year for re-tuning. If Phillips had discovered some small improvement in the meantime, this would have been incorporated into the soundbox before it was returned to the customer, so we cannot even be sure that the boxes which have survived are now exactly as they were when new. As in later years soundbox design became standardised, the old models would have been surrendered in part exchange against the new ones, and so the waste bins in the workshops would have filled up with obsolete models. When the war came, in the interests of the National Salvage Campaign, the bins would have been emptied, which accounts for the very sparse examples extant today. Also, as E.M.G. supplied soundboxes for customers who owned other makes of gramophone, we cannot even be sure that any surviving examples were originally supplied for E.M.G. machines, though it must be likely that at least some were.

If the exact progression of soundbox development remains partly shrouded in doubt, the reasons why the Exhibition box was chosen as the basis for the tuneable handmade box, are fortunately crystal clear. Design of the mass produced gramophone, as Balmain reminded us, was driven by the twin devils of 'foolproof cheapness.' The same applied to the soundbox. This resulted in a machine with an average to good reproduction, but which did irreparable damage to records. Those who wished to use fibre needles on a mass produced machine and soundbox found that not only was there a pathetically small volume, but that the points broke down early in the record. Thus, a hard choice was forced upon the keen gramophonist: if he wished to preserve his expensive records, he must buy a handmade soundbox.

Anyone who doubts that there was much of a skill in tuning a soundbox, or that there were more than a few variables that might need consideration, might be interested in part of an article in *The Gramophone* by Percy Wilson:

"Let us glance for a moment at the numerous variations possible in point of detail when constructing a soundbox of the Exhibition type. The back plate may be made from numerous substances; it may vary in weight, thickness and shape; in particular the distance its front face enters the front shell of the soundbox may vary, thus varying the distance between the back plate and diaphragm; further, the size of the central hole may be varied. The gaskets may be varied in thickness and elasticity. The upper arm of the stylus bar may be made from all sorts of metals - e.g. brass, bronze, phosphor bronze, soft iron, mild steel, it can be varied in shape, dimensions and weight, and its physical properties need not be uniform throughout - e.g. a soft, iron upper arm may be hardened at the tip, where it turns over to meet the diaphragm.

The needle socket also may be made from a variety of metals and varied in shape and weight; even the weight of the needle screw may be varied. The springs, apart from being tightened up or slackened, may be retempered; if necessary they may be replaced by another pair either weaker or stiffer, (and they may be scrapped in favour of one of the many other alternative spring mountings). The diaphragm may vary in weight or thickness, and within small limits, in diameter. Is it likely then that the tuning of these boxes can be a simple matter, when it may involve new gaskets, newly tempered springs, alterations to or partial or complete reconstruction of the stylus bar and possible operations on the back plate in a lathe? Is it so very surprising that commercial boxes of this type vary in quality?"

It was this very large number of variable factors that made the Exhibition the ideal subject for further experiment. Though it was generally an excellent box, it was not an unvaryingly good performer. At the 1925 Gramophone Congress Balmain's state of the art machine attracted criticism for the poor performance of its Exhibition box. David Phillips was quick to spot its potential, and much of his effort to improve its performance and balance it with the rapidly improving new exponentially correct acoustic systems was directed to trying to simplify it, and make it consistently reliable, whilst retaining its sensitivity. He was helped by three separate factors.

A.F.J. Wright's 'Meltrope back' patents gave him the soft rubber collar with compression ring, allowing him to abandon the clumsy Lifebelt flexible coupling. Virtz soundboxes tuned to a specific type of music gave him much insight into how to build tuneability into his own boxes. Finally, Harry Burden brought him the aluminium diaphragm. Burden had been playing about with aluminium ever since 1923 at least, but it was not until much later, about 1927, that he made the crucial discovery that it could be perfected by the simple expedient of pressing annular rings into it. When Phillips was first shown one of these diaphragms, and Burden suggested he should try it, Phillips just laughed at him. When he tried it though, the laughter died on his lips, it was exactly what he had been looking for. Burden was then hired to make diaphragms exclusively for E.M.G., and later, when the firm moved to Grape Street, Burden was employed full time for this specific purpose.

It was no small achievement then for David Phillips to design, assemble and tune his boxes so that not only were they outstandingly sensitive and effective, but that they would remain in tune for at least six months of hard use. This is reflected in the keen interest in these items when they appear in the auction houses today. Indeed, anyone who owns a gramophone and wishes to listen to music critically, will find that one of these boxes will add a nobility to the reproduction of all but the crudest machines.

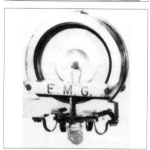

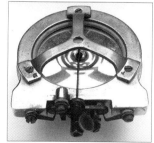

Appendix II - Horns

The horns used in the two types of Magnaphone were of vulcanite manufactured under A.T. Collier's patent 178,186 of 1921, and sold by him direct. It is not known who made the later vulcanite internal horns employed by E.M.G.

The Wilson Panharmonic Horns were mostly made by Scientific Supply Stores of Newington Causeway, S.E.11. They were made of alternating layers of blue and grey sugar paper, so that it was easy to count the layers required.

Paperdura of the Passage, Exmouth Street, Clerkenwell, E.C.11 also made Wilson horns, though it is not known whether they had Wilson's permission to do so. Their Wilson horns are identifiable by a final coating of block whiting over the top of the final coat of paper. This gave a smooth finish, which could then receive a finishing coat of either paint, or an appropriate paper.

Paperdura also made some of the Davey Isophonic horns, but it is not known if they made all. Expert horns were made also by this firm, but not exclusively as Pytram of New Malden, and Paper Designs (address unknown) also made them.

Appendix III - Acoustic Machines

This appendix is for general guidance only. As machines were available to private order, any combination of features was theoretically possible, though it is unlikely that many compromises were allowed in the acoustic systems. Most differences would have been in the finishes to the horns, veneers, and types of motor.

Details are given of machines at the dates of their introduction.

	1923-24 MAGNAPHONE	1925 E.M.G.
TONEARM	Seymour Sprung	E.M.G. Pivot Bearing-Goose neck with Quincke Tube
SOUNDBOX	Seymour Concert	Luxus or Jewel with E.M.G. Adaptor
HORN	Collier Patent Vulcanite 16" Round Bell or 12¼" x 6" Flattened Rectangular	Collier Patent Vulcanite 16" Round Bell
MOTOR	Thorens Model 'A' Triple Spring Model 'B' Double Spring Table Grand Double Spring	Thorens or Collaro (+£2)
CABINET	Solid Mahogany - Various Styles or Lacquer on Plywood or Chinoiserie Lacquer on Plywood.	Solid Mahogany
PRICE	Model 'A' £30 Model 'B' £25 Table Grand £16	De Luxe Cabinet £45 Model 'A' £30 Model 'B' £25 Table Grand £18

	1926 E.M.G. SUPER TABLE GRAND	1926 E.M.G. PEDESTAL MODEL
TONEARM	E.M.G. Pivot Bearing Type with Lifebelt and Weight Adjuster	(12/26) New Lighter Goose Neck with Quincke Tube
SOUNDBOX	Exhibition Type Conversion Brass Body, Mica Diaphragm	Exhibition Type Conversion Brass Body, Mica Diaphragm
HORN	E.M.G. Patent Alloy 12^1/$_4$" x 6"	Collier 12^1/$_4$" x 6" with Wooden Extension
MOTOR	Collaro D30 Double Spring	Any make supplied
CABINET	Solid Oak, Mahogany, Walnut or Teak	Solid Oak, Mahogany, Walnut
PRICE	Oak £14 Mahogany £15-10-0 Walnut £16-10-0 Teak £18	Oak 25 guineas Mahogany 27 guineas Walnut 30 guineas

	1927 E.M.G. WILSON HORN MODEL	1928 E.M.G. MARK VII
TONEARM	Inverted Pivot Bearing. Gooseneck Adjustable	New Longer Gooseneck Adjustable Quincke Tube
SOUNDBOX	E.M.G. Exhibition Type, or Meltrope or E.M.G./Meltrope	E.M.G. Exhibition Type with Meltrope Back (later E.M.G. Long Bar)
HORN	Wilson Panharmonic (Mark I)	270° Davey Ebonite
MOTOR	Paillard GGR 255 (HMV No 32 for Lumiere Conversion)	Paillard GGR 255
CABINET	Details Unknown Save Oak Box with raised Plinth to take inverted Tonearm and Horn (and Lumiere Conversion)	Veneered Ply, Various Designs in Oak, Walnut and Mahogany
PRICE	Oak 15 guineas	Oak £40 Mahogany £45 Walnut £50

	1928 MARK VIII	**1929 E.M.G. MARK IV**
TONEARM	E.M.G. Gooseneck with Quincke Tube + U Tube	Gooseneck Adjustable
SOUNDBOX	E.M.G. Exhibition Type, Mica or Aluminium Diaphragm with Meltrope Back (or Meltrope I)	Meltrope and E.M.G./Meltrope
HORN	50" Wilson Panharmonic Horn with 24¹/₂" Bell	'L' Shaped Papier Appliqué
MOTOR	Paillard GGR 255	Various Types Used
CABINET	Solid Oak with Dove Tailed Corners Solid Mahogany with Dovetail Corners De Luxe Model with ³/₄ Lid	Veneered Plywood
PRICE	Oak 15 guineas	Oak 12 guineas Mahogany Teak

	1929 E.M.G. MARK X	**1929-30 E.M.G. MARK V** (Mark VI believed identical but pedestal made with storage for 100 records beneath)
TONEARM	E.M.G. Gooseneck Adjustable	E.M.G. Gooseneck Adjustable
SOUNDBOX	E.M.G. Long Bar 4 Spring	E.M.G. Long Bar 4 Spring
HORN	Davey Isophonic 26/27" Bell	Large Internal - No Details Known Ebonite
MOTOR	Paillard GGR 255	Paillard GGR 255 or Collaro D30
CABINET	Table Model only Veneered Ply Quarter Cut (Oak) Ebonised Edges	Table Model No Details Known
PRICE	Oak £30 Mahogany £32 Walnut £35	Oak £25

	1930 E.M.G. MARK Xa	**1932 E.M.G. MARK IX**
TONEARM	Wilson Swan Neck	Wilson Swan Neck
SOUNDBOX	E.M.G. 4 Spring Brass	E.M.G. (Horseshoe Shape 2 Spring)
HORN	Davey Isophonic Papier Appliqué 28″ Bell Diameter	Davey Isophonic 22″ Bell Diameter
MOTOR	Paillard GGR 255 or Collaro D30 or Garrard Electric Induction	Collaro D30 Garrard U5 Electric
CABINET	Veneered Ply	Veneered Plywood
PRICE	Oak £30 Mahogany £32 Walnut £32	Oak 16 guineas Mahogany

	1933 E.M.G. MARK Xb	**1935 E.M.G. MARK XB (Oversize)**
TONEARM	Wilson Swan Neck	Wilson Swan Neck
SOUNDBOX	4 Spring Nickel Plated Brass	4 Spring Nickel Plated Brass
HORN	Davey Isophonic 29$^{1}/_{2}$″ Bell Diameter	Davey Isophonic 34″ Bell Diameter
MOTOR	Paillard GGR 255 or Collaro D30 or Garrard Electric Induction	Paillard GGR 255 or Collaro D30
CABINET	Veneered Plywood	Veneered Plywood
PRICE	Oak £32 (later available in Mahogany and Walnut)	Oak £35

	1930 EXPERT SENIOR	**1930 EXPERT JUNIOR**
TONEARM	Expert Gooseneck Adjustable	Expert Gooseneck Adjustable
SOUNDBOX	Expert 2 Spring (later 4 Spring) Brass	Expert 2 Spring or 4 Spring. Brass
MOTOR	Collaro D30	Collaro D30
HORN	28" Expert Single Bend Papier Appliqué. Plaster Coating (later Horns up to 36" and beyond offered)	As Senior but 24"
CABINETS TABLE MODEL	Veneered Plywood Cellulose Finish	Table Model only Veneered Ply Cellulose Finish (Later French Polish)
PEDESTAL MODEL	French Polish or to Special Order	
PRICE	Oak (Table Model) £32-10-00 Oak (Pedestal Model) £37-10-00	Oak £22-10-00 Mahogany £25 Walnut £27-10-00

	1930 EXPERT MINOR	**1932 EXPERT CADET (Later Ensign)**
TONEARM	As Senior	As Other Models
SOUNDBOX	Expert 2 Spring	Expert 2 Spring
MOTOR	Collaro D30	Collaro
HORN	As Senior but 18" Bell Diameter	As others. Originally 12" soon replaced by 18" Bell Diameter
CABINETS	Table Model only Veneered Ply Cellulose Finish	Table Model-Plain Box, No Lid Veneered Ply Cellulose Finish
PRICE	Oak £19-10-00 Mahogany £20	Oak only £12-10-00

TONEARM	Expert Gooseneck Adjustable
SOUNDBOX	Expert 2 Spring
MOTOR	Collaro D30
HORN	Twin Internal (Wilson/Webb) Design Bifurcated Tern Plate
CABINET	Veneered Ply Range of Colour Schemes Offered
PRICE	Oak £16-10-00 and Stand @ £2-10-00 but Mahogany, Walnut, Sycamore or Maple or Solid Teak, Brass Bound £20

Appendix IV - Cascade Machines

In the quest for perfect acoustical reproduction of recorded music, E.M.G. and Expert undoubtedly led the way. The machines they offered though were, scientifically speaking compromises. For true purity of science and reproduction a straight exponential system was required. In the judgement of both Ginn and Davey, no customer was likely to accept a straight horn which would have had to be in the region of nine feet long, hence the curved horns, which delivered the sound compactly, at a convenient height, and adjustable for direction.

W.J. Bond and Sons Ltd of Milton Avenue, Harlesden London NW 10 were also pilgrims on the same road. Plywood and timber merchants, and machine woodworkers, they produced gramophones from 1930 to 1940 as a sideline to their main business. Sideline it may have been, but when it came to acoustic science, they were fundamentalists. They would accept no bending of the rules, or the acoustic system merely to pander to aesthetics. They would produce the nearest approximation to a perfectly straight system that ingenuity could devise. Thus, the Cascade series of machines evolved. Starting with the sideboard gramophone which contained a straight horn, they progressed through the Cascade II to the Longhorn or Cascade III. The latter, surely the ugliest gramophone in the world, and vaguely suggestive of a cubist robotic granny with an outsize eartrumpet, was nevertheless of all the handmade gramophones, the one that contained the truest acoustic system. Whilst the Expert machines exceeded the E.M.G. in brightness and forwardness of tone, and the E.M.G. exceeded the Expert in refined and romantic expression, the Cascade gave its owner an extraordinarily faithful and delicate reproduction. At a basic price of only ten guineas, it was a tremendous bargain. Like the E.M.G. and Expert it bore the unmistakable stamp of Percy Wilson, who had designed the tone arm and the elbow, not to mention the mathematics of the horn. It should, if it was to receive its just deserts, have swept the board. It was though never destined to receive the favour of the higher echelons of the musical establishment and this must have been due entirely to its bizarre appearance. All of which goes to show that Homo Sapiens is not the rational creature he thinks he is.

The appearance of the E.M.G. and Expert machines, whilst they were at first greeted with amazement, on the whole attracted feelings of reverence and even awe. The Cascades with the external horns met open ridicule, and guffaws of uncontrollable mirth. In a strange way though, they acted as a sort of bench mark of comparison with their rivals. Any customer who went to look at all three makes, whilst he may have had doubts as to the domestic acceptability of the E.M.G. and Expert, when he saw the Cascade, found his former doubts evaporate.

Before we allow the memory of the Cascade machines to fade to the accompaniment of mocking laughter, we should do well to accord to them the honour of being probably the truest of all the acoustic systems, certainly the best value for money, and more important still, a machine that brought the high quality hand made gramophone within the grasp of impecunious enthusiasts.

Not much is yet known of W J Bond and Sons Ltd. They began business in 1920 and they were still going in mid 1940, but what happened to them thereafter is not known. I have a file of correspondence from W.W. Bond, then senior partner, to a customer covering the early part of 1940, in which Bond writes laconically;

'Please excuse the delay in replying to your post card. Things are rather difficult here at the moment, owing to the difficulties of getting materials, and the complicated system of regulations which now have to be observed....'

There is no mention of the nightly barrage or showers of bombs.

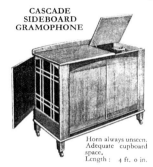

Finally a Cascade anecdote - too good to waste. The time was early 1930s when the Depression was at its nadir. There was a music master at a private boarding school who had been trying to persuade the school to purchase one of the hand made gramophones for the music department. He had recommended the E.M.G., but the school would only provide enough for a Cascade. As the master had himself been contemplating the purchase of a good machine for his own use at home, he hit upon the brilliant idea of approaching W.J. Bond and Sons to see if they would give a good discount if he was to buy two machines at once. In the course of conversation with one of the parents, a titled gentleman, he mentioned his clever idea. To his delight, he now found that this gentleman was also contemplating buying not one machine but two, one for his flat in the City, and the other for his house in the country. The idea now occurred to them that by combining forces, an order for four machines might attract an even bigger discount.

In due course they ventured to London to put their scheme to the test. It happened to be a pouring wet day. The streets were deserted. The showroom was also deserted, but there was a Cascade demonstration model for their inspection. After a time an elegant if lugubrious salesman appeared, and hovered. The titled gentleman, who had been elected leader for the day, came straight to the point. Banging his hand down on the lid of the Cascade, he asked:
"How much if we buy four of these machines? "

There was a stunned silence. The salesman, due to the dreadful state of the market had not sold a single machine for as long as he could remember. He was also accustomed to people coming in on wet days just to fall about with laughter at the machine's bizarre appearance. Thus he perceived that these two men were now having some new kind of joke at his expense. So, it was with some surprise that the two men saw the salesman roll his lugubrious eyes, and leave the room in apparent disgust.

It was not without some difficulty that they finally persuaded him to return. After profound apologies, and copious explanations, the deal was finally thrashed out, to the satisfaction of all parties, and W.J. Bond and Sons were able to chalk up their biggest one day sale ever.

Cascade Gramophones

Patent - 345813 and Patent applied for

WHY YOU SHOULD HAVE A GRAMOPHONE AND CHOOSE A GOOD ONE

THE MAGIC OF MUSIC With a gramophone you can bring into your home and have under your control one of the most magical and beautiful things in life - music. Practically the whole range is open to you. No matter what your tastes there are records which will delight you. It is not necessary to have a large number. The more the better of course, but a dozen or less are plenty for a full evening's concert.

EFFICIENT APPARATUS But for the finest results an accurately designed instrument is essential, as in all scientific and musical matters. Our Cascade gramophones, though far from being the most expensive are the finest gramophones that can normally be obtained. Theoretical and practical perfections have been incorporated to the highest possible degree, producing specially satisfying reproduction to critical musical ears.

FIBRE NEEDLES We consider these practically essential to those who take the gramophone seriously. The musical quality (with suitable soundbox) is better than can be obtained from steel needles, and they do not wear the record at all.

RADIO The wireless is not a substitute for your gramophone, but its complement. With the gramophone you control your own programmes.

ELECTRIC GRAMOPHONES are disappointing, even fairly expensive ones, from a musical point of view. The reproduction is artificial heavy booming bass and defective treble, and uneven and unstable generally. The Cascade gramophone is much more musically perfect, is so natural that it can be listened to by those used to good music indefinitely. It is not temperamental, practically trouble-free.

A SATISFACTORY OUTFIT AT A LOW PRICE. Anyone possessing a Cascade II gramophone with electric motor and special fibre soundbox at a total cost (delivered in London and district) has as fine an outfit as is ordinarily obtainable for playing gramophone records, and nothing better could be recommended to anyone taking up this fascinating interest.

THE PLEASURE to be derived from music increases indefinitely, and the necessary re-hearing can only be conveniently obtained by means of a gramophone - there is no substitute. The gramophone will soothe you when you are tired and worried, stimulate you to action, refine your whole mind. Many creative thinkers have stated that they use the gramophone as a means of thawing their minds. Whether it is for one of these purposes, or for learning a language or arranging a dance, you need a good gramophone on many occasions.

Please raise any points which interest you by letter, telephone, or better still call and hear the instrument for yourself.

Absolutely no obligation on you or pressure to buy. Bring your own records for test. Any time (including evenings and Saturday afternoon) if previous notice given.

GENERAL DESCRIPTION The single aim has been followed in designing this gramophone of attaining the highest possible degree of efficiency, combined with convenience and economy. The fine reproduction required calls for unending patience in experimenting, the use of the best components available and having some of them specially designed and made for the gramophone.

MOTOR This may aptly be described as the heart of a gramophone. It must have many good qualities such as strong pulling power, steadiness and silence. The motors we fit are the Collaro. The Collaro motor is a fine engineering job and is guaranteed for five years (springs one year). The spring motor plays four 12″ sides with one winding. Where A.C. current is available we recommend the electric motor (Collaro). There is one at 5s more and one at 5s less than the spring motor. (Consumption of current is negligible). It is guaranteed for five years. When ordering state current and frequency. These motors and any other components will be supplied separately.

Both the spring and electric motors are now supplied with a new pattern <u>automatic stop</u> which is very efficient and works with the run-out.

SOUNDBOX. At the price of £10 10s - (Cascade II) we include the Meltrope III soundbox (12/6), which we consider by far the best soundbox for steel needle playing. We strongly recommend, however, all those desirous of taking the gramophone seriously to use fibre needles, which give finer musical results without wear on the records which remain flawless indefinitely. To get really satisfactory results from fibre needles, however, it is necessary to have a well-designed gramophone, acoustically and mechanically as perfect as possible (such as the Cascade) but also a special soundbox.

Where, (as in the majority of cases where we supply a Cascade) it is proposed to use fibre needles we recommend that instead of supplying the Meltrope III (which is not then required) we supply our special tone-arm (as described below). As the extra cost of this is 12s. 6d the price of the gramophone is £10. 10s. plus the cost of whatever soundbox is selected. A Meltrope II specially altered by Mr. Wild for fibre costs £1. 1s. Specially made fibre soundboxes by various well-known makers who specialise in them are about £3. Any such soundbox ordered through us is of course specially tuned by the maker for the Cascade. It sometimes happens that a prospective purchaser already possesses a satisfactory soundbox. We are always willing in such cases to supply the gramophone without a soundbox, making of course, the full allowance.

TONE-ARM   This is of very fine design with gentle curves. By an invention of our own - a neat simple device - the tracking is reduced to under 2 degrees maximum. This very small error is so arranged that there is a plus error (under 2 degrees) where the record starts, the same error where it finishes, and a reverse (minus) error of under 2 degrees at a point 3.46″ from centre of record. It will be obvious that there must under this arrangement be two points (where the error changes from plus to minus and back to plus again) of zero error. In effect the soundbox is never more than very slightly off the ideal tangential position, and the tracking may from a practical point of view be regarded as perfect. The centre hinge is nearly square with the plane of the diaphragm, thus maintaining the vertical position of the soundbox with varying lengths of needle projecting. This centre joint is a well made job and works easily.

This standard tone arm is adequate for fibre needles. But with these latter it was felt that this bearing did not provide a sufficient margin of accuracy. Records vary enormously in the strain put upon the needle point, and as stated above to get the best results from fibre needles the very finest mechanical perfection is needed. We have, therefore, designed a special base, which is used in tone-arms on machines intended for fibre needle playing. It incorporates a ball-bearing of finest British make, a piece of high grade precision engineering work. The balls and races are glasshard and guaranteed to be true to 1/10,000″ both as regards size and sphericity. In order to ensure air-tightness, and also to protect the bearing from dust and damp it is sealed both top and bottom by the device of a circular tongue running in a channel filled with soft grease. The result is a bearing of delightful easy and even movement, which will give perfect action indefinitely.

ELBOW Bends present the greatest difficulty in gramophone design. Sound naturally travels in a straight line, and there is a risk of breaking up the delicate wave formation in getting round corners. (The waves are best visualised as circular discs of energy passing along the sound conduit from soundbox to horn mouth and expanding, of course, with the increasing diameter of the sound conduit. In the tone-arm there is not much risk as the diameter is small and the energy consequently concentrated. But when the diameter becomes large and the energy is consequently attenuated, its form is easily broken up. In its endeavour to travel in a straight line it strikes the side of the horn - if this is not a dead straight one as in the Cascade (part of its energy is absorbed in the material of the horn) and so causing unwanted horn resonances and the remainder is reflected at the angle of incidence. A rough visual idea of what happens can be seen when a stone is dropped into the centre of a pond. The train of waves starts (taking any part of the circle) straight for the edge of pond. The waves remain perfectly clear and distinct until they meet some opposing object. Waves are then reflected and form a criss-cross pattern with the first series. The ear is particularly sensitive to purity in wave form.

Returning to our elbow. It involved a turn where the diameter is about 1¹/₂". This is not very large, but we wanted even this dealt with in the best possible manner and we were fortunate enough to get the aid of the leading mathematical gramophone expert in this country to design this part. The mathematical perfection of this elbow contributed a great deal to the purity and "marvellous forwardness" to which Mr. Compton Mackenzie has referred. The elbow is heavily cast in brass.

HORN After the elbow there are no bends, for the horn is dead straight, there is no further obstruction to the straight path of the expanding sound waves. The material is papier-mâché. In the Cascade II the hardwood end of the horn is turned to form a perfect fit with the elbow so that the sound-conduit is continued smoothly and there is no possibility of leakage. The horn is simply pushed in and out as required. It is strong, but light and easy to handle and can be hung on a loop of string if desired to keep it out of the way.

The whole sound-conduit has been designed as a whole to give an unbroken steadily expanding air column. One of its most important features is the dead straight horn ("The only true exponential horn is the straight horn"- P. Wilson M.A. in *The Gramophone*".)

Those interested in the technical side of gramophone design will recognise the possibilities of a gramophone designed like the Cascade. Its performance fully justifies all the care taken to bring it at every point to the highest possible degree of perfection.

CABINETS It is convenient to consider these separate from the acoustic aspect of the gramophone, but it would be a mistake to suppose that they are not an integral part of the design. Actually one experiments first with all sorts of scaffolding, but as the design becomes more definite the cabinet comes into existence with it, until there is presented in the Cascade cabinets objects which are at once beautiful, convenient and efficient for their purpose.

SIDEBOARD MODEL The horn is completely concealed and never seen as Compton Mackenzie says "it really is what it claims to be" a very well made sideboard. The aperture of the large horn is at the side so that every inch of the generous cupboard space can be utilised. Its value for money is truly remarkable". It is made in finest quality oak.

CASCADE II (External Horn Model). This is of very neat design, a delight to the eye. The horn is black dappled with gold, and is just slipped in and out as required. When out, a polished disc covers the hole. It is well made from perfect hardwood and well French polished. The various parts are made from special materials specially selected for each purpose. The record cupboard door though not thick or heavy, will not warp, being made from a laminated board. The motor board is of very heavy multiplywood to give maximum strength at this important part. Special attention has been given to ensure strength and rigidity throughout, as this is a most important thing in a gramophone. The large cupboard will take about 150 12" records in covers. A small panel at the top slips out to make it easy to dust the motor board. The cabinet can be made in special hardwoods at small extra charges.

As the Cascade II stands in a room its appearance is superior from an artistic point of view to heavily ornamented instruments. With the horn inserted it does look a little unusual at first (the quality of the reproduction is also decidedly unusual), but this is not to say that it is unsightly. It is in fact quite neat and compact with the horn inserted, and the small mental adjustment necessary is quickly and unconsciously made. Some concession (and this is a very small one) should be made to the conditions necessary for perfect reproduction. A small folded horn must be inferior. No one would insist that all the instruments of an orchestra should be perfectly rectangular. They are allowed to assume the shapes which best suit their purpose. A grand piano is not so compact as an upright one, but those who can, have the grand. It is the same with the Cascade gramophones. The sideboard is large, the Cascade II has an external horn, but this is the price of quality.

Please write, telephone (Willesden 2825) or call if you would like further information. Demonstrations at practically any time.

THE CASCADE III GRAMOPHONE

ITS CHIEF FEATURE The outstanding and distinctive feature of a Cascade Gramophone is its dead straight horn. Our rule in designing was "The best that can be done at each point". The dead straight horn is universally agreed to be the ideal, because soundwaves are naturally propagated in straight lines, square to their plane, and are broken up and lose their energy when, as in bent horns they meet opposing surfaces. (Gentle bends in the tone-arm do not matter as here the energy in the soundwaves is compact and they keep their form - it is where they are expanded that damage is easily done. In Cascade III the waves are expanded at mouth to 3, 000 times their digital area.) The Cascade gramophones have only one bend after the tone-arm in the sound-conduit - the elbow specially designed by P. Wilson, M.A. it is a right angle and the diameter is only 1¹/₂". Other machines have several other bends, and what is worse, have them in wider parts of the horn.

THE CASCADE III therefore, with its sound conduit of nine feet over-all has a dead straight horn with mouth of 28" and a neat support near the mouth to take its weight. It is not heavy and can be easily handled by one person. When not in use it can be hung vertically (mouth upwards) in a loop of string on a nail in any out-of-the-way corner, with ease, without the slightest inconvenience to anyone. The cabinet then looks neater than an ordinary gramophone.

CASCADE II OR CASCADE III In deciding which of these instruments to purchase it should be remembered that the larger horn model requires over 7 feet long of floor space to accommodate it. It therefore calls for a fairly large room to use conveniently. Regarding reproduction, it must be understood that the improvement is not in proportion to the increase in size - although the exponential horn increases rapidly in size as it is developed, there is a rapidly diminishing return in improved reproduction. In small rooms Cascade II will sound perfectly satisfactory. The extra cost of Cascade III over Cascade II is £2 10s. A Cascade II can be converted into a Cascade III at any time by the purchase of the larger horn.

COMMERCIAL GRAMOPHONES The Cascade is in an entirely different class from the ordinary commercial instrument designed and made for the majority. The difference is often described as startling by those who hear it for the first time.. This does not exclude electric gramophones. The "radio-gramophone" may be impressive; by reason of its "punch" when one first hears it, but one soon tires of the unnatural reproduction. They are still very much in the experimental stage and become obsolete a few months after purchase. The Expert Committee of *The Gramophone* said of one which cost £70 by a leading maker:

"we miss a certain delicacy and refinement of touch - one gets that in the best acoustic gramophones. We have not yet been satisfied in this respect by any commercially produced radio-gramophone. We must confess to a feeling of disappointment."

IF YOU HAVE A CRITICAL EAR for fine music, buy the Cascade. It is more naturally musical in tone than any other gramophone; and because of its straight horn gives a purity and forwardness of reproduction which is unique. It cannot easily get out of order and is therefore trouble free. If you use fibre needles as we recommend you can build a library of records which will remain perfect indefinitely (this cannot be done with steel needles). It is a pedestal instrument, so there is no need to buy a table and record cupboard as well. Finally, though extremely well made of best quality material, it is sold at a very low price. Altogether a great bargain from every point of view. Come and hear it.

TRACKING ERROR An important point in gramophone design. If the needle is to engage accurately in the fine groove of the record and do its work with maximum ease and efficiency, the plane of the soundbox should be tangential (square with radius) to circle of groove at the point where needle touches it. A departure from the ideal angle of 90 degrees will cause the needle to point across the groove and so into the side of it, causing, with steel needles, damage to the record. Strain is set up at the needle point by this geometrical defect. With fibre needles the tendency of this strain is to break the needle point.

Apart from the effects on needles and records, it is clear that the backward and forward motion of the diaphragm, corresponding to the wave form of groove, is more efficiently effected with the plane of diaphragm tangential with the groove.

If the soundbox could be moved across the record in a straight line it would be easy to put the soundbox tangential and keep it so, but its path is necessarily curved, with the consequence that at some points its angle with the radius is greater or less than the ideal of 90 degrees. The amount of variation is the tracking error. For successful use of fibre needles, and to reduce record wear with steel needles to reasonable limits, maximum tracking error should be under 5 degrees. With our device it is possible to reduce it to under 2 degrees. Graphically the curve of error would be nearly straight, with two points at zero, so that in these conditions the tracking error can reasonably be regarded as negligible.

How to effect the alteration. We require to be supplied with one or two measurements (instructions for taking which we give) and from these we set the matter out geometrically, and ascertain the way in which the tone-arm falls short of the ideal. We then make carefully a device to the exact size necessary to correct this error and bring maximum tracking error under 2 degrees. The device is light, perfectly neat and well finished, and easily slipped on and off.

It may be necessary for you to make a small alteration in the position of the motor relative to tone-arm base. (We supply the measurement). When considering the matter it is advisable to look ahead to see whether this can be done conveniently. Also as our device is an extension of the tone-arm at soundbox end it may not be possible to shut the lid down with tone-arm folded back when the gramophone is not in use. To render this unnecessary we supply a tone-arm rest in such cases.

Out charge is 10s. and includes all necessary instructions, working out each case geometrically, preparing device to special size, and providing tone-arm rest where necessary.

We will of course advise where we think the alteration not suitable and return any remittance in full.

Write, telephone (Willesden 2825) or call to discuss the matter

We are behind the Harlesden (Bakerloo - L.M.S.) station - take four first left turns. Almost any time suitable.

FIBRE NEEDLES The two great advantages of playing gramophone records with fibre needles are:

(a)   Complete absence of record wear (the most serious defect of steel needles) with flawless reproduction indefinitely.

(b)   An all round finer quality of musical tone.

The perfection of modern recording and gramophone design (of which the Cascade is an outstanding example) makes it possible to bring the illusion of listening to an original performance to a very high pitch. But nothing destroys this illusion so much as the defects in the records which steel needles soon produce. Why then are not fibre needles in general use? The reason is that with ordinary gramophones they are not successful as a rule. They are not sufficiently finely designed, the moving parts of the tone-arm are not sufficiently free and the tracking error not low enough, so that the fibre needle point is broken before the record is finished. (With steel needles it is the record which breaks down.) Moreover to get the best results with fibre needles a specially made soundbox is necessary.

With a properly designed gramophone such as the Cascade with a suitable soundbox fibre needles are a brilliant success. It is only necessary to observe a few simple conditions.

SOUNDBOX. A specially tuned Meltrope II soundbox costs 21s. Specially made fibre sound-boxes may be obtained at 35s. and 65s. They are made by those who have specialised in them and are specially tuned in each case by the maker to suit the Cascade.

DRYNESS OF FIBRES It is generally only necessary to re-sharpen a fibre needle after every few records. The sharpening is the simplest possible instantaneous process. The cutter costs 4s. and must of course be sharp. It has been found that the needles give better results if kept dry and this is most conveniently done by keeping the packet of needles in a tin of calcium chloride. A 1lb airtight tin can be obtained from Boots Cash Chemists for a few pence. The tin should be kept closed except when a needle is being taken out or put in.

RECORD SURFACE   It is important that this be kept scrupulously clean. It should be brushed both before and after playing. A suitable brush costs 1/9. It sometimes helps with heavy recordings to sprinkle a very little fine graphite on the surface and brush it in, or a sharpened good quality pencil may be used to lubricate the grooves. Records to be played with fibre should not be played with steel. Even a few playings may be sufficient to spoil it from the fibre point of view. Note: Buy your records from shops which only use fibre or insist on having new copies Winter note: See that surface of record is perfectly dry, free from atmospheric damp.

LOW TRACKING ERROR Low tracking error is important and that of the Cascade is practically ideal. The angle of the stylus bar should be 55 degrees, (we provide a protractor) and needle projection about $\frac{3}{8}$".

GET A CASCADE GRAMOPHONE and Play your records with FIBRE NEEDLES. You will thus get the greatest pleasure that gramophone records can offer. You could not have a better outfit.

<u>Basic Price of Cascade II</u> Gramophone with Collaro D30 spring motor, Standard (II) horn, tone-arm with precision ball-bearing, mercury seal, extension for low tracking error and stabiliser (weight adjusting) but <u>without</u> soundbox   £12 17s. 6d

<u>Cabinet</u> Extra for cabinet in oak £1 10s.   Mahogany £2 0s.
          Teak   £2 10s.   Walnut   £2 10s.

<u>Soundboxes</u> Expert Standard -   £1 15s.   Expert Dynamic   £3 5s.
          Meltrope III (steel needles) 12s. 6d.   Meltrope IIIa (B.C.N.) 17s. 6d.

<u>Larger Horn</u> (III) with support, <u>in lieu of</u> Standard Horn £2 15s. 0d.
Extra for bakelite finish to horns. Standard 5s. Larger 10s.

<u>Electric Motors</u> (Collaro) Empire A.C. 5s Universal A.C.-D.C. 10s. extra.
(State voltage and frequency of current & length of flex)

<u>Tone-arm</u>, for precision ball-bearing in non-corrodible steel instead of ordinary steel
                                                           - 15s. extra.

Sundries   E.M.G. Fibre needle cutter -   5s. 0d. (Davey)
                Expert   "   "   " -   6s. 0d. (E.M. Ginn)
                B.C.N. needle sharpener   -   5s. 0d. (Meltrope)
                Fibre needles (Expert) pkt. 50   2s. 0d.
                Glydola graphite record polish   1s. 3d.
                Record brush (Expert) -   1s. 9d.
                Calcium chloride (1lb. in
                        airtight tin)   9d.
                Heavy grease for horizontal
                        joint of tone-arm   -   6d.
                Handbook Gramophones acoustic
                        and radio (P. Wilson)   1s. 0d.

<u>Packing Cases</u>   Not charged for if returned promptly in good condition. Should be consigned on return as "Returned empties" for economy. Each gramophone requires two cases, one for cabinet and one for horn.
        Case for cabinet   3' 6" x 2' 0" x 1' 8" (Weight)   1½ cwt   17s. 6d.
          "   " Horn II   3' 6" x 2' 3" x 2' 3"   (with)   1   "   17s. 6d.
          "   " Horn III   6' 6" x 2' 7" x 2' 7" (contents) 1½   "   35s. 0d.

Cases are of course charged for overseas orders. The particulars given above should enable those overseas to ascertain cost of freight, etc. Wherever possible we prefer overseas purchasers to make their own arrangements regarding carriage.

<u>Carriage</u> is extra to above prices. Small parcels must be prepaid, complete gramophones are sent carriage forward. Average cost of carriage, including returning crates, in England 12s.6d. In <u>London</u> and district (including London Docks) we deliver complete gramophones free by our own motor.
    Nearest railway station should be stated.

    Any parts of our gramophones will be supplied separately.

Appendix V - Select List of Patents

107,262	Seymour	1916-	Superphone principal
103,904	Russell and Seymour	1917-	Fibre needle holder
177,215	C.L. Balmain	1922-	Horn gramophone
178,186	Collier	1922-	Vulcanite horns
290.469	A.F.J. Wright	1928-	Soundboxes stylus bar mounting
297,559	A.F.J. Wright	1928-	Soundboxes Meltrope back
298,330	A.F.J. Wright	1928-	Soundboxes stylus bar/diaphragm
312,524	A.F.J. Wright	1929-	Soundboxes stylus bar mounting
318,356	A.F.J. Wright	1929-	Pick-up arms (mounting)
322,663	Wireless Music Ltd.	1929-	Needletrack alignment
332,238	Wireless Music Ltd	1930-	Loudspeakers
340,525	EMG/Darrieulat	1930-	Record storage
346,852	Wireless Music Ltd	1931-	Sound recording/reproducing
357,578	Ginn and Phillips	1931-	Gramophone design - Expert accoustic system
377,467	Wireless Music Ltd	1932-	Vibratory Devices
481,051	E.M.G./Maltby	1938-	Improvements in talking machines
509,428	H.B. Davey	1939-	Loudspeakers
601,531	E.M.G./F.G.G. Davey	1948-	Improvements in circuits
615,786	E.M.G./H.B. Davey	1949-	Improvements in sound reproducers
638,563	E.M.G./F.G.G. Davey	1950-	Needle sharpener (Rollright)
661,715	E.M.G./F.G.G. Davey	1951-	Filter Circuits (steep cutting filter)
688,644	E.M.G.	1953-	Burglar Alarms
704,779	E.M.G.	1954-	Burglar Alarms
713,542	E.M.G.	1954-	Burglar Alarms

Provisional Patents, later abandoned:
14553 The Magnaphone Patent.
June 2nd 1923.

7774 Sound reproducing apparatus March 9th 1929 (E.M.G. Centrelock)

Acknowledgements

Books of this nature are usually the product of a co-operative effort. Though the name on the cover is that of the author who harvests all the credit and all the brickbats, in reality, the covers enclose material that is the literary property of other people, and a great deal of information which has been freely given by yet more people.

This little venture would have been impossible without the unqualified co-operation of *The Gramophone*. To A.C. Pollard therefore, who has kindly permitted reproduction of all the material I wished to use, I offer my most grateful thanks. He also helped by giving me the vital introduction to Joe Ginn, and supplying such historical material as he could find in *The Gramophone* archives. James Jolly, editor of *The Gramophone*, also allowed me to clutter up his office for a whole day, and Quita Chavez provided valuable reminiscences of days at E.M.G. during the early part of the war, so many thanks are also due to them.

Joe Ginn, (pronounced with a hard G as in gracious) the last surviving link with Expert gramophones, gave me the Ginn side of the story, which occupied many days of his precious time, and even more evenings on the telephone. We have both enjoyed our mutual voyage of re-discovery, and without his selfless help and encouragement, this book would have been impossible

To Peter and Jane Davey I also owe a great debt of gratitude, for they provided much detail of the Daveys' side of the story, and illustrations on pages 29 and 34.

To Christies South Kensington I am particularly grateful for permission to use photographs from the sale catalogues, on pages viii, 32, 33, 35, 44, 53, 71 and 108.

The National Magazine Company kindly allowed me to reproduce two photographs from *Harpers Bazaar* and to quote from an article therein.

Mrs Diana Boston provided the photographs of Mrs Lucy Boston and her Expert Senior on pages 84 & 85, and welcomes visitors to the Old Manor, Hemingford Grey by appointment (Tel: 01480 463134).

The British Museum newspaper library at Colindale permitted the reproduction of the advertisements from the *Brighton and Hove Herald*, and an article therefrom.

I wish to record my gratitude also to Horace West. His invaluable help in reconstructing the events leading up to the split of Michael Ginn from E.M.G. as well as memories of the firm stretching back to the day in May 1930 when he was first appointed a director, have provided insights that have proved crucial in unravelling many mysteries. He kindly provided the photograph on page 36.

To John A. Job, the last managing director and partner in E.M.G., I am most grateful for permission to use the famous E.M.G. trademark on the cover, and elsewhere.

To Mark Wickham I am indebted for the picture of his father, on page 66, and the photograph of his father's Mark Xb on page 80.

Roger Thorne gave me the benefit of his help and advice, hundreds of photocopies from his extensive library, and discovered the Seymour Superphone, just in time for its picture to be included. More than these however, I am grateful for his ever cheerful and enthusiastic encouragement.

I have needed a lot of encouragement to keep this venture on the rails, and of those who gave it, no one gave more than Alastair Murray, who did the drawings of various premises, derived from poor photographs taken in London on a pouring wet day. I am as grateful for his constant encouragement, as for his masterly drawings on pages 11, 38, 52 and 77.

Ted Perry provided the photographs of himself with other members of the E.M.G. staff on page 98.

Howard Hope generously provided the photographs of the Expert Minor on page 54, and the Cascade III on page 120.

Much of the photography has been done by Anni Sommer, always at inconvenient times, and usually to meet impossible deadlines. She has done it well, and must have starved on the little she charged for it.

It has taken me three years to collect and check and organise this material into a form which I hope will prove acceptable. This is all time that should have been spent on the farm. If it had not been for my poor wife struggling away all this time alone, we should now be reaping a grim harvest of death among the live-stock and a plague of thistles in the fields.

The fact that the stock is healthy, and the fields cleaner than they have ever been, suggests a state of affairs I do not want to think about! Clearly much of the credit for the appearance of this book lies with my wife, Jan.

Finally there is the host of others, friends, complete strangers, and members of my family who have helped with research I was unable to undertake for reasons of time or distance, and this book is theirs as much as it is mine. If I have omitted anyone, their only consolation will be that this will cause me more grief than it will them - I hope.

Brian A'hearne
Paul Austwick
Keith Badman
John Booth
Harold Burtoft
British High Commission Dar es Salaam
Keith Catchpole
Major Edward Creese
Patrick Crouch
Doug Dowe
Eddie Dunn
Andrew Gainey
George Frow
Gilbert Fury
W.C.C. Gaymer
Glos. Library Service
Alan Haughton
P. Heath
Ted Hock
Hugo Hodge
Mrs J. Holmes
Dave Homewood
H. Huxley
John Isherwood
Capt. Charles James MBE, MA
Mrs J.L.B. James
Dr. T.B. James MA. Phd. FSA
R.F. James
James Jolly
Mrs Rachel Kalis
Andrew Keener

Peter Larner
Phillip Lewis
Don Lock
Miles Mallinson
Ian Maxted
David Mitchell
Michael Morgan
Frank Mulvaney
Enid & Nigel Mummery
George Overstall
Richard Parkes
Jo Pengelly
Michael Penny
Christopher Proudfoot
Nikki Rowan-Kedge
Dr. Boris Semeonoff
Eric Smith
Peter Stinson
Richard Taylor
Sir Richard Turnbull K.C.M.G.
Don Watson
W.J. Watson
Joseph Wherrett
D. White
Eric Whiteway
Michael Wickham
Christopher Woolard

Index

A

Amis, J. 84
Apollo 18

B

Balmain, C.L. 3, 12, 13, 16, 107, 108, 124
Balmain gramophone 12, 13, 24
Barnett, H.T. 24
Barnett, Samuel and Sons 37
BAW Syndicate 37
Behrend, R.H. & Co. 48
Bentham, J. 35
Berners, Lord 56, 58, 59, 78
Binaural Listening 90
Bond, W.J. 65, 66, 77, 114-123
Boston, Mrs. L *85*
Boult, A. 93
Bourne & Tant 11
Bradley 9
Bratley & Overstall 85
Brayne, R. 57, 66, 80
Bromley, Bob 77
Burden, H. *18*, 108
Burne Jones 91

C

Carpenter, R. 34
Cary T. 97, 98
Chaplin, C. 58
Chaplin, S. 58
Chavez, Q. 83, 85, 125
Cinetra 38
City Accumulator Company 63, 69
Clarke, S.C. 15
Coates W. 68
Collier, A.T. *5*, 20, 109, 110, 124
Columbia 6, 24
Compton Mackenzie 11, 13, 15-16, 18-19,
    23-25, 74, 75, 83, 119
Constantinescu, C.C. 36
Creese, E.J. 18, 19, 49, 59, 63, 69

D

Darrieulat, F. 31, 38, 41, 42, 45, 69, 124
Davey, Baron 29
Davey, Jean 105
Davy, H. 5
Decca 37
Delius 34, 35, 76
Disque Cabinet Co. 14
Donatti 78
Duer, S. 91
Duophone 37

E

East London Gramophone Society 23
Edwards, 63
Electrical & Mechanical Gramophones Ltd.
    38
Electrogram 62
E.M.I. 57
Evans, E. 68
Exhibition of British Industrial Art 68
Expert Committee 25, 34, 43, 49, 54-5, 62-3,
    65-6, 77, 121

F

Faraday, M. 5
Fenton, T.G. 48, 83, 84, 93, 96
Foss, H. 93

G

Gas Purification Group 91
Gilman, L. 16
Godfrey, F.E. 62, 69, 71, 77
Gramophone Company 6, 28
Gramophone Congress 17, *18*, 18, 19
Gramophone Exchange 81
Green, G. 40-44
Grundig 91
Guest & Merriman 24

H

Hancock, T. 5
Harrison, H.C. 24
Harrods 39
Hatry Case 36
Henson, L. 58
Hichens Harrison 36, 37
Hill, H. 38, 47, 76, 77
Hill, M. 86, 89
H.M.V. 24, 25, 27, 28, 29, *35*, 74, 79, 85, 94,
    110
Hyperion Records 97

I

Imhofs 97

J

Jewel Soundbox 17, *17*, 109
Job, J.A. 93, 97, *98*, 101-105, 125
John, A. 80

K

Kalisch 13
Keener, A. 104

L

Lawrence, T.E. 75, 81
Layton, R. 104
Leach, 78, 79
Leak, H.J. & Co. 88
Lewis, D. 97
Lewis, E. 36, 37
Lifebelt 23, 108, 110
Little, H.F.V. 16
Lockhart, R.S. 93, 100-105
Lutyens, E. 59
Luxus soundbox *17*, 17, 18, 116

M

Maltby, F. 71, 83, 124
Mann, Judd & Gordon 95
Mantovani 80
Marles Steering Gear Co. 36
Maxfield, J.P. 24
Melhuish 85
Meltrope 62, 76, 108, 110, 111, 118, 122-124
Merriman & Guest 24
Metcalf-Casals, S. 79

N

Norris, Teddy 96

O

Ogden, C.K. 35, 36, 37, 39, 58, 67
Orchosol 18, 57, 61
Orthophonic Victrola 24
Overstall, G. 85

P

Paper Designs 109
Paperdura 109
Parsons, G. 83, 84, 85
Perry, Ted *95*, 97, *98*
Phillips, B. 2, 3, 19, 23, 37
Phillips, J. 2, 8, 19, 49
Phillips, L. 2, 19
Pollard, A.C., vi, *99*
Prowse, K. 61
Pytram 109

R

Reah, J. *95*, 97
Red Cloud 78
Rendall, Reverend, H. 94
Rendall, M.J. 94
Richmond & District Gramophone Society 39
Rimington Van Wyck 74, 75
Rosebery, Countess of 56
Rothermel, Crystal 88

S

Scientific Supply Stores 25, 109
Serpolet Steam Car Co. 36
Seymour, E.V. 6
Seymour, H. 3, 4, *5*, 5-7, 11, 14, 16, 17, 22, 23, 124
Seymour, R. 6
Shaw, G.B. 39
Shirley, J. 97-8
Sitwell, E. 67-8
Sitwell, O. *59*, 60, 76
Sitwell, S. *59*, 59, 60, 76
Slater, V. 97
Somerbell, C. 69
Sopwith, T.O.M. 79
Sorabji, Prof. K. 54
Sound Wave 11, *13*
Steinway Hall Tests 12-15
Stone, C. 14, 15, 38
Stranger, R. 63, *63*
Swinnerton, F. 4

T

Telefunken 79, 83
Thynne, Lady B. 56
Trouton, M. 34

V

Vallin, N. 76
Vesper Gramophone 6
Virtz 108
Voxhaus 70

W

Webb, G.W. 3, 16, 70
Webbs Radio 91
Wells, M. 58
Welte-Mignon Player Piano 12
Wenderland 22
West, H.E. 35, *36*, 36, 37, 40, 42-45, *48*, 50, 125
West, H.H. vii, *48*, 48, 50, 82, 95, 103, 104
Wickham, M. 66
Wild, W.S. 16
Wilkes & Co. 77
Wilson, G. 77, 78, 79
Wireless Music Ltd. 34, 124
Wolsey Television 91
Wood, E. 80
Wright, A.F.J. 108, 124

Y

Young, H. 97
Young, L. 13, 14

Reference to illustrations in **bold italic**

Illustrations

E.M. Ginn	iv
Magnaphone 1924	viii
Seymour Superphone	5
267 High Holborn, W.C.1.	11
Seymour/Wilson tonearm	17
E.M.G. Stand at Gramophone Congress	18
Bronze Medal	19
Balmain Gramophone	24
First E.M.G. Wilson Combination	26
Two early E.M.G. soundboxes	28
Horace Balfour Davey	29
Mark VII E.M.G.	32
Mark VIII standard	33
Mark VIII de luxe	33
Captain F.G.G. Davey, M.A.	34
E.M.G. Mark VIII conversion	35
H.E. West	36
Grape Street, W.C.2.	38
E.M.G. Prototype Mark X	39
Darrieulat's Serpentine Chest	41
E.M.G. Mark IV	44
Davey Radiogram DR5	46
H.M. Bateman's sketch of the Wests	48
55 Rathbone Place	52
Expert Senior	53
Expert Minor	54
Mark Xa	58
Osbert & Sacheverell Sitwell	59

E.M.G. Mark IX 1932 — 60

Salon Decca converted to E.M.G. Xb — 61

Michael Wickham — 66

Some E.M.G. publications of the 1930s — 67

Two Mark Xbs — 68

The Wilson/Webb bifurcated horn system — 70

E.M.G. Xb Export Model — 71

E.M.G. XB oversize horn — 72

Expert All Range horn — 72

E.M.G. XB oversize — 73

64 Frith Street — 77

Expert Pipe Organ Radiogram — 78

Michael Wickham's E.M.G. Mark Xb — 80

Stuart Lockhart with a DR7 — 81

Expert Senior at the Manor, Hemingford Grey, 1942 ... — 84

... and with Mrs. Lucy Boston — 85

Michael Ginn, R.N. — 86

A selction of Expert products — 89

A.C. Pollard of *The Gramophone* with David Phillips — 91

A selection of E.M.G. accessories — 94

Interior of Newman Street — 95

Newman Street Record Counter — 98

E.M.G. Staff — 98

26 Soho Square — 105

Tailpiece — 106

Soundboxes — 108

Cascade III — 120